Lote Tree Learning

+1 832- 378-7365

hello@lotetreelearning.com

www.lotetreelearning.com

Ordering Information:

Quantity sales. Special discounts are available on quantity purchases by corporations, associations, and others. For details, contact us at the address above.

Printed in the United States of America

First Edition

Illustrations by Israa Alaa Ismail

ANCIENTS

History
Connections
Book 1
Middle Grades

SUMAIA B. MICHEL, DRS
SARA MAGDY

Lote Tree
LEARNING

READ THIS FIRST

We know, reading the introduction is often boring and you would rather skip it! We promise to keep it as short as possible! Reading through the parts below will save you time later on, when you are doing the lessons.

As you can see, we were messing around with some paint while making this book, and so you will find some splatters and drops here and there. We hope this will not hinder you when learning about history.

ELEMENTS

You *could* skip this part, or you could read it and have an overview of what we aim to do with all the different parts in the lesson. If you wish to skip this, go straight to the 'How to Use this Book' part. In every lesson there are several elements, which are summarized in the Task Card on the first page of every weekly lesson:

WEEK: 1	CREATION		
RESEARCH:	Creation, Prophet Adam (as) Idrees (as)	RESOURCES:	UILE HI Super Servant Stories
SKILL:	Outlining	PROJECT:	Poster
MAPPING:	Creation	TIMELINING:	Adam (as)

Research

Learning how to read and understand a scientific text is an important life-skill. It helps create life-long and independent learners. In the Research box of the weekly Task Card, the key words are listed. You are encouraged to find the topics in the encyclopedia by yourself, by using the content pages or the index pages. The keywords listed help you in finding the topics in the encyclopedia.

Resources

We have listed the resources that will be used for the week in the resources section of the weekly Task Card. UILE stands for the Usborne Internet Linked History Encyclopedia, HI stands for History Intersections, 2nd edition and the Super Servants Stories are optional.

Skill

The program covers a wide range of skills, including outlining, summarizing, note-taking and mind mapping. These skills are not only useful for the subject of history, but are life-skills to be used throughout a wide range of subjects, both academic as well as non-academic. The difficulty of the skills will be increased over several weeks, allowing you to become proficient through small incremental steps.

Project

Every week, you will create a project: sometimes this is with pen and paper and sometimes this is with an online software. The purpose of the project is to show information you have found in a visual manner. You will practice a project for several weeks, so you can become really good at it. When making posters, we use canva.com. This is a free website that allows you to make posters and other graphics. You can go to the website and set up a free account. For the Powerpoint presentations, we will start using Prezi.com. Prezi allows you to choose a dynamic template. Once done with your presentation, save it and you can share the link with anyone you like to show your work. Again, this is a website where you can set up a free account.

Map

You will make a map by tracing a Location Map and following the instructions every week. The instructions will tell you what items should be marked and labeled on the map. The map should be made with colors and have as much details as possible. Every map should be labeled at the top with the topic of the week. The purpose of having you trace the map is recognition of topographical landmarks and elements such as mountain ranges, rivers, deserts, seas, oceans, and cities. By physically tracing a map, the information is integrated into your memory. Most Location Maps are traced more than once. You will find all the maps in the Maps & Rubrics booklet.

Timeline

Timelining involves the placement of information in chronological order on a visual that represents the passage of time. Most timelines are linear, starting from one point and moving in one direction. Such timelines will give a good sense of the order events are happening in, and which events happen at the same time. However, a linear timeline does not show the different topographical areas things happen in at the same time. Therefore, our timeline is circular: it is shaped like a slice of a tree trunk, with the rings showing its years. We have also divided the circular timeline in 'slices', like a pizza. Every slice represents a different area of the world. When data is added to the timeline, all events happening in the same rings are happening at the same time, and going from the center to the outer ring in each slice, will show the order of events for that particular area.

Every week, you will write the chronological information found (and if applicable, the dates in the boxes in the resources,) on the timeline in the topographical area the events took place in. Not only time matters, but also place. See instructions below on how to assemble the timeline.

World Wall Map

In order to have a sense where events on the traced map take place on a global scale, we will ask you to locate the traced map area on the World Wal Map. The World Wall Map is a complete world map without details. See instructions below on how to assemble the World Wall Map.

HOW TO USE THIS BOOK

When you start, look at the Task Card at the beginning of the weekly lesson. It will list the topic and the keywords that will help you find the pages in the resources that you will need. The resources are listed as well.

First you will need to get the resources needed, then you will open the content page and see if you can find the pages that talk about this topic. You can also use the index in the back of most resources. Sometimes the pages are easy to find, and sometimes it will take you some searching. The most important thing is to find ALL pages related to the topic.

Secondly, read through the lesson pages, so you have an idea what is expected from you. It would be a shame if you spend a lot of time reading and writing down things, while at the end you find out that was NOT what you were supposed to do. No one likes to waste time.

Then, you will start reading the pages in the resources, using the directions under the 'Research' part and the instructions in the 'Skill' part. Outline, summarize or take notes as directed. Once you are done with that, the first day, you will work on the Map and Timeline, and the second day, you will do a Project. Sometimes, the project might take a bit of time. That is alright, the more time you spend, the better your project will be. The skills and projects are abilities that you will use the rest of your life, even after your school days are over.

The book is set up in such a way, that the skill and project increase in difficulty over time. Every week, the information is repeated and new information is added. In order to make sure you do not miss the new information, look for the 'New' paint blotch next to the text.

In the back of the book, under Appendix, we have added a few pages that we think may help you. We have listed a cheat sheet for the research questions, a list of Roman Numerals and the Color Wheel. You can take these pages out and keep them next to you while reading or working on your project. Or not: whatever suits you best.

PROPOSED SCHEDULING

This curriculum contains 30 weeks of history lessons. We recommend doing your history twice a week, and we have divided the lessons in two days for this purpose. We do not recommend doing this subject only once a week, as the resources will require time for reading and notetaking etc. For teaching history more than twice a week, we have given an example schedule below.

Please plan for 45 minutes to complete the activities on each day. There may be times where this is significantly less, or more, because the project might take time, depending on your skill level.

Proposed Schedule – Twice per week

DAY 1	DAY 2
• Read the pages in the resources (use the directions under Research) • Skill (outline, summarize or take notes, according to instructions) • Map • Timeline • (Start your project if time allows)	• Read the pages in the resources (use the directions under Research) • Skill (outline, summarize or take notes, according to instructions) • Project

Alternate Schedule – Four times per week

DAY 1	DAY 2	DAY 3	DAY 4
• Read the pages in the resources (use the directions under Research) • Skill (outline, summarize or take notes, according to instructions)	• Map • Timeline • (Start your project if time allows)	• Read the pages in the resources (use the directions under Research) • Skill (outline, summarize or take notes, according to instructions)	• Project

BEFORE YOU START

Before you start this program, assemble the World Wall Map and the Tree Trunk Timeline according to the instructions below.

Prepare the World Wall Map before the first lessons. Remove the pages for the World Wall Map from the Maps & Rubrics booklet, and keep them in order. Place them in front of you, image upwards, in landscape format. Cut off the right and bottom part of each page, as neatly on the line as possible, keeping them in order. Turn the pile upside down, and start with the page now on top. Place this page on a surface in front of you, to the bottom right, with the image upwards. Turn the next page over and place it to the left of the first page, overlapping the white border of the first page and aligning the image. Do the same with the next page and the fourth one: now the lower row is completed. Place the fifth page on the top of the first one, overlapping the top white border of the first page and aligning the image. Place the sixth one to the left of the fifth one, overlapping the top white border of the second page and the left white border of the fifth one, and align the image. Continue until all four rows (each four pages) are completed. Use a glue stick or white glue to stick all pages together. Assemble the Tree Trunk Timeline in a similar manner as the World Wall Map.

We recommend hanging the map on a wall where you can easily see it, as this serves as a visual reminder. It is important when tracing a map, you have an understanding what part of the World Map you are tracing. You can use your hands to form a rectangular frame, the way photographers do, when you demonstrate the geographical area on the World Wall Map that is being discussed.

Should you prefer not to hang the posters on the wall, you can assemble them and add them to a foam poster board. Attach the World Wall Map on one side and the Tree Trunk Timeline on the other side. This way you can put the map and timeline away, and bring it out whenever you need it.

RUBRICS & CHECK-LISTS

We have provided you with all rubrics and check-lists that we have placed in the parent manual as well. Look at the rubrics in the Maps & Rubrics booklet before you start a project, because it will help you understand what is expected of you. The check-lists help you look at your own work when you have finished, and see if you have included the elements necessary.

There you have it; that wasn't so bad, now was it? If you have any questions, you can always message us on facebook messenger! (Make sure your parents know about it too.)

CONTENT

LESSONS

WEEK: 1	CREATION		
RESEARCH:	Creation, Prophet Adam (as) Idrees (as)	RESOURCES:	HI Super Servant Stories
SKILL:	Outlining	PROJECT:	Poster
MAPPING:	Creation	TIMELINING:	Adam (as)

EXPLANATION

TOPIC: CREATION

Learning about history is very important because it explains why things today are the way they are. On top of that, it helps us understand problems and why they happened, so hopefully we can learn from them.

Allah (swt) often uses stories of people from the past in the Qur'an so we can learn from them. He (swt) mentions 25 prophets and their stories in the Qur'an. This year, we will cover 22 of their stories.

We will start at the beginning: The Creation of Humankind. Read the Story of Adam (as) and Idrees (as) from the History Intersections, second edition. Additionally, you can read the story of Musa (as) from Super Servants Series stories.

RESEARCH:

Day 1:

When reading a scientific text, such as from an encyclopedia, we need to learn how to take the information from the text. A good way of doing this is by asking yourself questions before, during and after you read.

Let's start by looking at questions we can ask ourselves **before reading** a text:

*   What do I want to learn?
*   What do I think the topic is about?

Jot down some short sentences or words to answer these questions in your notebook.

From now on, you do not have to write down the answers to these questions. These questions should be in your head and you should ask yourself these questions honestly, and try to find an answer for them. If you feel writing down some answers helps you think about these questions, you can do so, of course. You just do not *have* to.

By time, you will find they help you quickly read and understand the text, saving you a lot of time and helping you hand in better work.

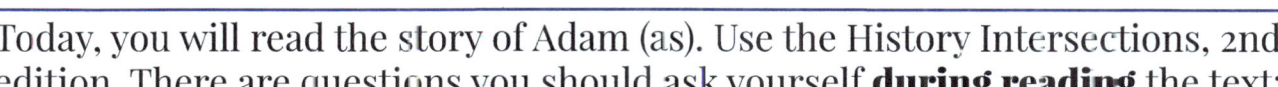

Today, you will read the story of Adam (as). Use the History Intersections, 2nd edition. There are questions you should ask yourself **during reading** the text:

- What is the writer trying to tell me?
- What is important?
- What happens next?

Day 2:

Today we will read the History Intersections, 2nd edition. Again, we will look at questions we can ask ourselves **before reading** the text:

- What do I want to learn?
- What do I think the topic is about?

You will use the History Intersections, 2nd edition today. Pay special attention to the first and last sentences in a paragraph: often the most important information is in one of these. These sentences are called **topic sentences.**

There are also questions you should ask yourself during reading the text:

- What is the writer trying to tell me?
- What is important?
- What happens next?

TIP: Dates and names are VERY important in history!

When we read a page in the encyclopedia or any other scientific text, the purpose is to extract the important information and then **write it down.**

We write stuff down for several reasons. Firstly, we remember it better if we write it down and secondly, we can always go back to our own notes and see what was the most important information. This helps us understand materials and study better.

Outlining means you write down the most important topic of every paragraph and you number them by Roman numerals. The topic of the paragraph is usually mentioned in the first or last sentence of the paragraph, but not always, so make sure you do read the entire paragraph! Use phrases or very short sentences to write the caption of each Roman numeral.

THE FIRST SETTLERS: c. 10,000 BC -5600 BC

The First Farmers

The very first people hunted wild animals, caught fish and gathered nuts, plants and berries to eat. It was thousands of years before people learned how to farm.

Farming began in the Middle East, in an area we call the Fertile Crescent. Around 10,000 BC, the weather there became wetter and warmer, so plants could grow more easily.

Cutting wheat with a tool called a sickle

People noticed that seeds which had fallen on the ground grew into plants. They began to collect the seeds and plant them on purpose. The first crops grown like this were wild wheat and barley.

These pots were made by early farmers.

Once people knew how to farm, they no longer needed to move around to hunt for food. They began to settle down in villages and learned how to make bricks from mud and clay to build homes.

In this picture of an early village, one house has been cut away to let you see inside.

Map of the Fertile Crescent

Fertile Crescent

A wall protects the village from wild animals.

Clay for building a new house

Well

Let us look at the page snap-shot. It has 4 paragraphs and a few images. We read each paragraph and write down the main point. Each main point has a Roman numeral. Go ahead and read the first paragraph, and then have a look at the main point written in the outline below. Do you think that this is indeed the main point of the paragraph?

Now, go ahead and read the second, the third and the fourth paragraph and look at the main point for each in the outline below.

So our outline will look something like this:

I.   The First people hunted and caught fish
II.   Farming started in the Fertile Crescent
III.   They planted seeds on purpose
IV.   People began to settle down

This is called a basic, or first level outline.

Each Roman Numeral lists one topic. In this case it lists the main topic of the paragraph. Every topic is indented: moved a bit to the right. When you write in your notebook, simply start the numeral a bit to the right. If you use a computer, you can use the Tab key on your keyboard to do this. Word program might do this automatically when you place a roman numeral and press the enter key.

When you have read each paragraph and written down the main point for each, do not forget to have a look at the images on the page. You might find important information in the image, which you simply add as another roman numeral.

TIP: If you do not know the Roman numerals, or you might need a bit of a reminder, please see the list in the back.

Your Turn:
Outline the Story of Adam (as) in a basic outline. For every paragraph, write down one main point, listed with roman numerals.

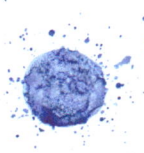

Posters are used to draw attention to a topic or to help understand and remember information. You will use posters to do the latter: understand and remember information.

The reader should look at your poster and understand the topic of the poster and the information regarding the topic.

There is a difference between a poster, an info-poster and an info-graphic. A poster has one single message: it could be an invitation, a reminder, a call to action (Buy This!) or a slogan.

An info-poster lists a bit of information around one message. With an info-graphic it is all about the information: it lists a lot of information. The most important part is the message.

You will make a **poster**: a poster with one message and a graphic or image to support that message.

We will look at the following elements of a poster:

- The Title & Subtitle
- Graphics
- White Space
- Colors

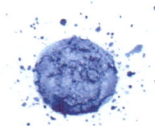

Title:

Your title should tell the reader what your poster is about. Do not use more than two lines for your title. Use 48 point size of the font (the letters) and use them in bold (fat).

This is 48 point size, in bold:  **Title**

A subtitle tells you a bit more about the topic in one short sentence. The subtitle is usually written in a smaller font, directly under the title.

Let us have a look at an example. Since we use posters to understand and organize a bit of information from our research on a historical topic, we will

pick only a few topics from our outline. Remember the basic outline we made?

Based upon this outline, we created this poster on Canva. We used one of their poster designs. We chose the design because it allowed us different parts, as the poster was already divided into one main part, and three smaller parts.

What is the title and topic of this poster?

Where is the subtitle?

Your Project:

Have a go at making a poster yourself! Log in to canva, and choose the poster templates. Pick a design you like for the topic of this week.

What design fits the story of Adam (as) well?

What would be a great title for this poster? Can you include a sub-title?

Requirements of poster: A premade poster template. Replace the title with your own. Add a subtitle. Delete information on the poster you do not need. The graphic or image of the poster has to fit the theme of the Story of Adam (as). Colors can be adjusted.

MAP:

Trace the map where Adam (as) & Hawwa landed on earth and eventually settled. Can you find the area on the world wall map? You can use the map on this page to help you find it.

Once you have traced it, mark the following:

- Where Hawwa landed
- Where Adam (as) landed

Make sure your map is labeled.

TIMELINE:

Mark Adam (as) on the timeline. This should be easy, as he was the beginning of human history!

Pay attention to the location: every 'slice' of the Tree Trunk Timeline is designated for a different continent. First find the 'ring' with the correct dates. Then, find the location you need. Write the information in that ring under that location.

TIP: When using your timeline, we advise you write with marker so your entries are easy to read.

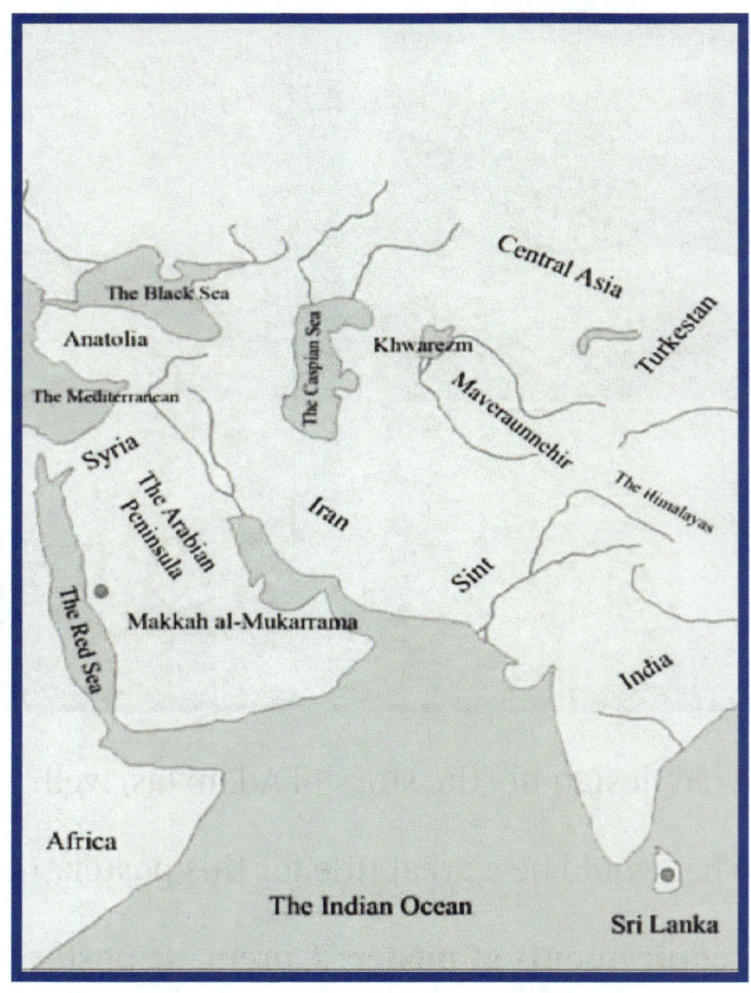

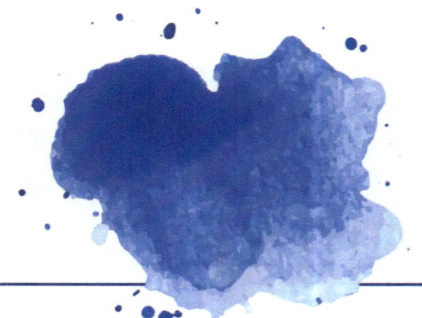

WEEK: 2   **FIRST SETTLEMENTS**

KEYWORDS: From Hunting to Farming, First Farmers

RESOURCES: UILE

SKILL: Outlining

PROJECT: Poster

MAPPING: Fertile Crescent

TIMELINING: First Settlements

EXPLANATION

TOPIC: FIRST SETTLEMENTS

Early humans were nomadic hunters. Nomads are people who wander/roam around and live in tents. The first farmers lived in the best area for farming; near two big rivers, the Tigris and Euphrates. The weather is wet and warm so it is very good for plants. People noticed seeds fall on the ground and sprout plants, so they started to sow these plants themselves. Once people knew how to farm, there was less need to move around to hunt. They learned to make bricks from mud and clay to build homes. One of the oldest towns found was Jericho.

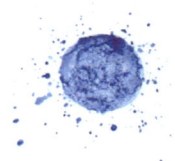

RESEARCH:

Day 1:

Today you will use the encyclopedia. Start by opening up the index page. We are studying the Ancients: where can you find topics regarding the ancients? Scan the topics list under ancients: where do you think you could **find information** for your topic? Open up the page of the topic.

A good habit is to scan the headings and sub-headings in a text to have an idea what the text is talking about.

So in summary, ask yourself the following questions when looking for the information:

In which book can I find information? What page in this book?
What are the pages in the book about? (Scan the headings and sub-headings)

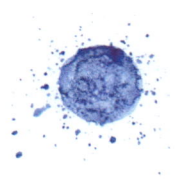

RESEARCH:

Day 2:
Continue reading in the Encyclopedia.

Ask yourself the questions **before reading:**

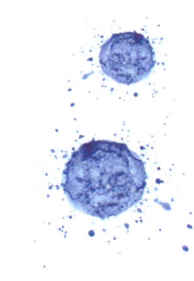

- What do I want to learn?
- What do I think the topic is about?

- In which book can I find information?
- What page in this book?
- What are the pages in the book about?

Then ask yourself the questions **during reading** the text:

- What is the writer trying to tell me?
- What is important?
- What happens next?

Outlining means you write down the most important topic of every paragraph and you number them by Roman Numerals. The topic of the paragraph is usually mentioned in the first or last sentence of the paragraph, but not always, so make sure you do read the entire paragraph! Use phrases or very short sentences to write the caption of each Roman Numeral.

Your outline should look something like this:

I.   The First people hunted and caught fish
II. Farming started in the Fertile Crescent
III. They planted seeds on purpose
IV. People began to settle down

This is called a basic, or first level outline.

Each Roman Numeral lists one topic. In this case it lists the main topic of the paragraph. Every topic is indented: moved a bit to the right. When you write in your notebook, simply start the numeral a bit to the right. If you use a computer, you can use the Tab key on your key-board to do this. Word program might do this automatically when you place a Roman numeral and press the enter key.

SKILL:

When you have read each paragraph and written down the main point for each, do not forget to have a look at the **images on the page**. You might find important information in the image, which you simply add as another Roman numeral.

TIP: If you do not know the Roman numerals, or you might need a bit of a reminder, please see the list in the back.

Your Turn:

Outline the topic of this week. For every paragraph, write down one main point, listed with Roman numerals.

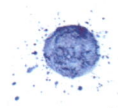

We will look at the following elements of a poster:

- The Title & Subtitle
- Graphics
- White Space
- Colors

Title:

Your title should tell the reader what your poster is about. Do not use more than two lines for your title. Use 48 point size of the font (the letters) and use them in bold (fat).

This is 48 point size, in bold: **Title**

A subtitle tells you a bit more about the topic, in one short sentence. The subtitle is usually written in a smaller font, directly under the title.

Graphics:

The graphics you choose, have to make sense with the topic: they have to be related to each other. Choose high resolution graphics, over 300 ppi. You can find beautiful images on websites such as pexels.com or pixabay.com or freeimages.com. If you use images that are not free to use, always mention the source. You can do this by placing small text between brackets under an image.

If you use a table or a figure, always make sure you use a caption (a title for the figure or table).

TIP: be careful when browsing the web searching for images. Make sure you stick to the mentioned websites, because sometimes when you download an

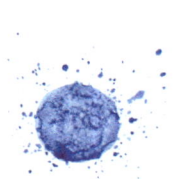
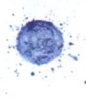

FIRST FARMERS

FARMING STARTED IN THE FERTILE CRESCENT

image, there is a computer virus attached to it and it will infect your computer.

Let's have a look at our poster again. We searched for images, and found the main one. We added three more smaller images with the same theme: so they all seem to fit together.

Your Project:
Which graphics would go really well with this topic? Explore the different images and elements on Canva. Pick the graphics that fit the topic for this week well.

Requirements: Pick a pre-made template based upon the parts of the poster needed. Add/remove parts as necessary. Title and subtitle should be correct. Image/graphics should match the topic.

TIP: either choose all pictures to use in your design, or choose all drawn elements, as mixing these up often creates a messy feeling.

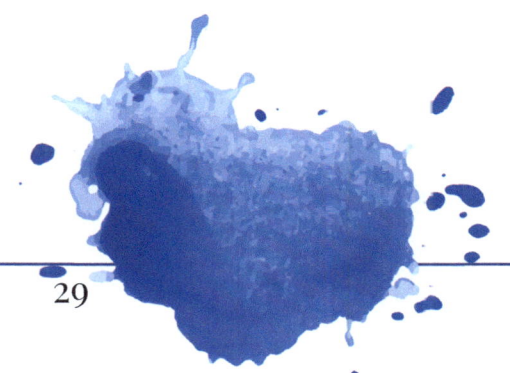

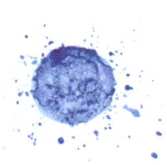

MAP:

Find the Fertile Crescent on the World Wall Map. Find the map you need to trace. Trace the outlines on your map.

Mark the following on your map:

- Trace the River the Euphrates and the Tigris.
- Color the rivers blue, and label them corrrectly.
- Color the oceans & seas
- Label the oceans & seas

Make sure your map is labeled correctly.

Use the map in the encyclopedia to help you.

TIMELINE:

Add First Settlements to your time-line.

The topics in this program are taught in order, so add this topic after the topic from last week. However, pay attention to the location: every 'slice' of the Tree Trunk Timeline is designated for a different continent.

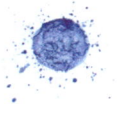

WEEK: 3	FERTILE CRESCENT & STORY OF NUH (AS)		
KEYWORDS:	Fertile Crescent, Mesopotamia, First Towns, Prophet Nuh (as)	**RESOURCES:**	UILE HI Super Servants Stories
SKILL:	Outlining	**PROJECT:**	Poster
MAPPING:	Map of Prophet Nuh (as)	**TIMELINING:**	Prophet Nuh (as)

EXPLANATION

TOPIC: FERTILE CRESCENT & STORY OF NUH (AS)

Slowly the small farming villages grew into towns. The oldest town found is Jericho. Jericho grew rich by trading with other communities. The largest of the early towns was Catal Huyuk. It had brick houses and the people made clay sculptures.

Day 1:
Read about the first settlements in the Fertile Crescent.

Day 2:
Read about Nuh (as) and the great flood.

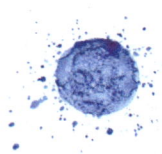

RESEARCH:

Day 1:

Today you will use the encyclopedia. Remember how to **find information:** Start by opening up the index page. We are studying the Ancients: where can you find topics regarding the ancients? Scan the topics list under ancients: where do you think you could find information for your topic for this week? Open up the page of the topic.

A good habit is to scan the headings and sub-headings in a text to have an idea what the text is talking about.

Ask yourself the questions **before reading:**

- What do I want to learn?
- What do I think the topic is about?

- In which book can I find information?
- What page in this book?
- What are the pages in the book about?

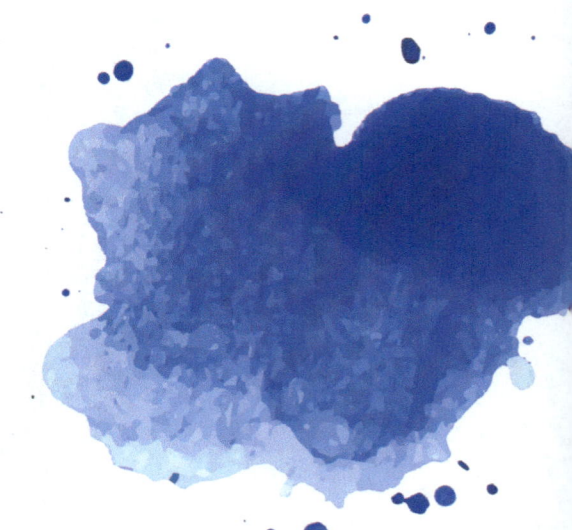

Now, look at the text, and **write down all difficult words:** this could be a word that you have never seen before, a word you find hard to read, or a word you do not know the meaning of.

Write down the difficult words from the text in your note book, like this:

Word: **Meaning**:

-
-
-
-

When you have written down these words, see if you can **find the meaning** for them. You can do this by asking someone, using a dictionary or looking it up on an app. Write the meaning next to the difficult word.

Then ask yourself the questions **during reading** the text:

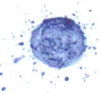

- What is the writer trying to tell me?
- What is important?
- What happens next?

Day 2:

Today you will read from the History Intersections, 2nd edition about prophet Nuh (as). Write down any **difficult words** with their meanings.

Ask yourself the questions **before reading:**

- What do I want to learn?
- What do I think the topic is about?

- In which book can I find information?
- What page in this book?
- What are the pages in the book about?

Then ask yourself the questions **during reading** the text:

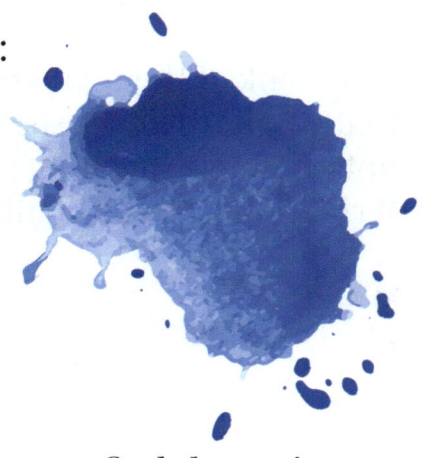

- What is the writer trying to tell me?
- What is important?
- What happens next?

SKILL: OUTLINING

Make a basic outline, using the research questions to help you find the main points.

Your Turn:

Outline the topic of this week. For every paragraph, write down one main point, listed with roman numerals.

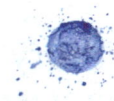

PROJECT: POSTER

We will look at the following elements of a poster:

- The Title & Subtitle
- Graphics
- White Space
- Colors

Title:

Your title should tell the reader what your poster is about. Do not use more than two lines for your title. Use 48 point size of the font (the letters) and use them in bold (fat)

This is 48 point size, in bold: **Title**

A subtitle tells you a bit more about the topic, in one short sentence. The subtitle is usually written in a smaller font, directly under the title.

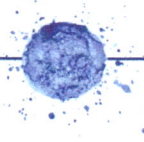

Graphics:

The graphics you choose, have to make sense with the topic: they have to be related to each other. Choose high resolution graphics, over 300 ppi. Do not use graphics from the google search page: these are always too blurry. You can open the graphic on the source page and save it from there. You can also find beautiful images on websites such as pexels.com or pixabay.com or freeimages. com. If you use images that are not free to use, always mention the source. You can do this by placing small text between brackets under an image.

If you use a table or a figure, always make sure you use a caption (a title for the figure or table).

TIP: be careful when browsing the web searching for images. Make sure you stick to the mentioned websites, because sometimes when you download an image, there is a computer virus attached to it and it will infect your computer.

Let's have a look at our poster again. We searched for images, and found the main one. We added three more smaller images with the same theme: so they all seem to fit together.

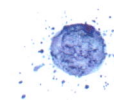

PROJECT:

Every week, you are required to save the template and your design, or different versions of your design. You can do this by selecting 'posters' in the template list. Then select the template you like to use from the left hand menu. It will appear on the white page on the right side of your window. If you look right above this poster on the right side, you will see a little sign of two pages on top of each other. Click this and it will copy the page with the template. You will leave the first page with the original template, and then use the second one to create your design. If you are required to create multiple versions, repeat this step and keep each version as a separate page.

When you are satisfied with your design, download all the pages (you have to select them in the upper right corner menu for download) as a pdf, so you can hand these in for evaluation.

Your Project:
Which graphics would go really well with this topic?

Explore the different images and elements on Canva. Under 'photos' you will find images and under 'elements' you can find all kinds of things needed, like shapes, lines, drawn images, art etc.

Pick the graphics that fit the topic for this week well.

Requirements: Pick a pre-made template based upon the parts of the poster needed. Add/remove parts as necessary. Title and subtitle should be correct. Image/ graphics should match the topic.

TIP: either choose all pictures to use in your design, or choose all drawn elements, as mixing these up often creates a messy feeling.

MAP:

Find the Fertile Crescent on the World Wall Map. Find the map you need to trace. Trace the outlines on your map.

Mark the following on your map:

- Trace the rivers The Euphrates and the Tigris blue.
- Label the rivers
- Color the oceans and seas and label them
- Locate where Ur would be and mark it on your map.
- Mark with a brown circle mount Judi.

Use the map on this page to help you find it. Make sure your map is labeled correctly.

TIMELINE:

Add Prophet Nuh (as) to your time-line.
The topics in this program are taught in order, so add this topic after the topic from last week. However, pay attention to the location: every 'slice' of the Tree Trunk Timeline is designated for a different continent.

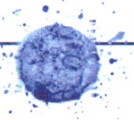

WEEK: 4	**SUMERIANS & AKKADIANS**		
KEYWORDS:	Sumer, Akkad, First Cities, Mesopotamia, Ziggurat, Crafts & Trade, Kings & Wars	**RESOURCES:**	UILE
SKILL:	Outlining	**PROJECT:**	Poster
MAPPING:	Mesopotamia	**TIMELINING:**	Sumer & Akkad

EXPLANATION

TOPIC: SUMERIANS & AKKADIANS

The farmers settled between Tigris and Euphrates. This area became known as Meso-potamia (this means 'land between two rivers' in Greek: meso-= middle, pota = river). The flat land of Sumer, one of the cities of Mesopotamia, was good for farming but had little rain. Akkad was another city. Sargon was the ruler of Akkad. He is also known as Nimrod, and we will learn more about him next week.

RESEARCH:

Day 1:

Today you will use the encyclopedia. Remember how to **find information:** Start by opening up the index page. We are studying the Ancients: where can you find topics regarding the ancients? Scan the topics list under ancients: where do you think you could find information for your topic for this week? Open up the page of the topic.

A good habit is to scan the headings and sub-headings in a text to have an idea what the text is talking about.

Ask yourself the questions **before reading:**

* What do I want to learn?
* What do I think the topic is about?

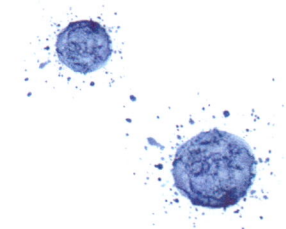

* In which book can I find information?
* What page in this book?
* What are the pages in the book about?

Now, look at the text, and write down all **difficult words:** this could be a word that you have never seen before, a word you find hard to read, or a word you do not know the meaning of.

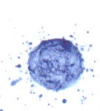

Write down the difficult words from the text in your note book.

When you have written down these words, see if you can find the meaning for them. You can do this by asking someone, using a dictionary or looking it up on an app. Write the meaning next to the difficult word.

Then ask yourself the questions **during reading** the text:

- What is the writer trying to tell me?
- What is important?
- What happens next?

Day 2:

Continue reading in the Encyclopedia. Write down any **difficult words** with their meanings.

Ask yourself the questions **before reading:**

- What do I want to learn?
- What do I think the topic is about?

- In which book can I find information?
- What page in this book?
- What are the pages in the book about?

Then ask yourself the questions **during reading** the text:

- What is the writer trying to tell me?
- What is important?
- What happens next?

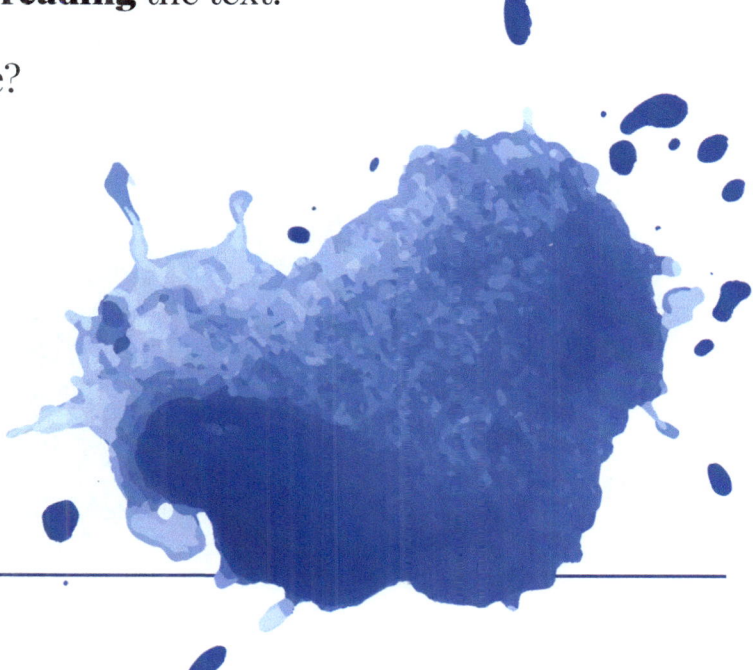

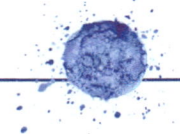

Make a basic outline, using the research questions to help you find the main points.

Your Turn:

Outline the topic of this week. For every paragraph, write down one main point, listed with roman numerals.

What are some really interesting facts you learned about the Sumerians and Akkadians?

Make sure you mention these in your outline as well!

PROJECT: POSTER

We will look at the following elements of a poster:

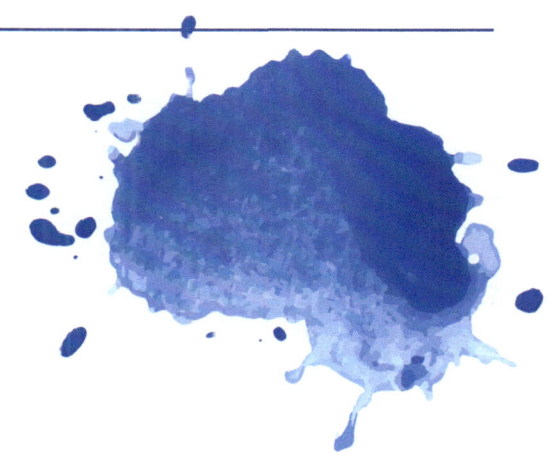

- The Title & Subtitle
- Graphics
- White Space
- Colors

So far, we have looked at title and graphics of a poster.

Title:
Your title should tell the reader what your poster is about. Do not use more than two lines for your title. Use 48 point size of the font (the letters) and use them in bold (fat). A subtitle tells you a bit more about the topic, in one short sentence. The subtitle is usually written in a smaller font, directly under the title.

Graphics:
The graphics you choose, have to make sense with the topic. Choose high resolution graphics, over 300 ppi. If you use a table or a figure, always make sure you use a caption (a title for the figure or table).

TIP: be careful when browsing the web searching for images. Make sure you stick to the mentioned websites, because sometimes when you download an image, there is a computer virus attached to it and it will infect your computer.

Whitespace:
This is one of the **most important** aspects of poster design: the space you leave 'empty'. It is not actually white: it can be any color or even part of an image. Whitespace means there is no text. This empty space helps create borders around text, helps organize the information in useful blocks and gives the viewer 'breathing space'.

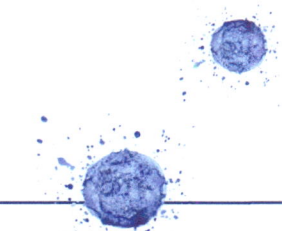

Let's have a look at our poster again.

Can you find whitespace?

Notice how the space between the images creates a border: this is also whitespace.

Every week, you are required to save the template and your design, or different versions of your design. When you are satisfied with your design, download all the pages (you have to select them in the upper right corner menu for download) as a pdf, so you can hand these in for evaluation.

Your Project:
Make a poster for the topic of this week, and pay special attention to **whitespace**: where is whitespace important in your poster? Make several versions with different whitespace areas and see which one you like.

Requirements: Pick a pre-made template based upon the parts of the poster needed. Add/remove parts as necessary. Title and subtitle should be correct. Image/graphics should match the topic. Whitespace should be used correctly: a minimum of three versions with different whitespace usage are made.

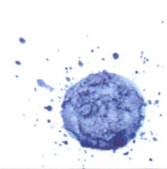
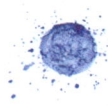

MAP:

Trace a map of Mesopotamia. Where on the World Wall Map can you find Mesopotamia? Which map will you need to trace?

Mark the following:

- Label the two rivers
- Label the oceans and seas
- Mark Sumer and shade it
- Mark Akkad and shade it, with a different color

Use the map in the encyclopedia to help you mark these on your map.

Make sure your map is labeled correctly.

TIMELINE:

Add Sumer and Akkad to your timeline.

Use the box with dates in the encyclopedia to add more events to your timeline. Remember to pay attention to location.

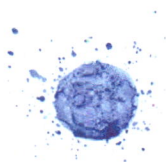

WEEK: 5	**PROPHET HUD (AS) & SALEH (AS)**		
KEYWORDS:	Prophet Hud (as), Prophet Saleh (as)	**RESOURCES:**	HI
SKILL:	Outlining	**PROJECT:**	Poster
MAPPING:	Map of Prophet Hud (as) & Saleh (as)	**TIMELINING:**	Prophet Hud (as) & Saleh (as)

EXPLANATION

TOPIC: PROPHET HUD (AS) & SALEH (AS)

Prophet Hud (as) was sent to the people of 'Ad and prophet Saleh (as) was sent to the people of Thamud. Both of these groups of people were blessed with wealth and prosperity. And both refused to believe and were detroyed.

RESEARCH:

Day 1:

This week, you will use the History Intersections, 2nd edition.

Remember how to **find information.** Scan the headings and sub-headings in a text to have an idea what the text is talking about.

Ask yourself the questions **before reading:**

- What do I want to learn?
- What do I think the topic is about?

- In which book can I find information?
- What page in this book?
- What are the pages in the book about?

Write down the **difficult words** from the text in your note book, and find the meaning for them.

Then ask yourself the questions **during reading** the text:

- What is the writer trying to tell me?
- What is important?
- What happens next?

Day 2:
Continue reading your resources. Write down any **difficult words** with their meanings.

Ask yourself the questions **before reading**:

- What do I want to learn?
- What do I think the topic is about?

- In which book can I find information?
- What page in this book?
- What are the pages in the book about?

Then ask yourself the questions **during reading** the text:

- What is the writer trying to tell me?
- What is important?
- What happens next?

We will now have a look at questions you can ask yourself after you have read a text.

- Did I understand what I read?

If you feel you did not understand everything very well, just reread the part you did not understand. Maybe there is a word that you do not know: find the meaning for the word and the text might become clear!

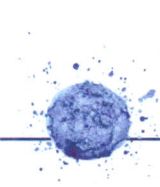

SKILL: OUTLINING

Make a basic outline, using the research questions to help you find the main points.

Your Turn:

Outline the topic of this week. For every paragraph, write down one main point, listed with roman numerals.

PROJECT:

We will look at the following elements of a poster:

- The Title & Subtitle
- Graphics
- White Space
- Colors

So far, we have looked at title and graphics of a poster.

Title:

Your title should tell the reader what your poster is about. Do not use more than two lines for your title. Use 48 point size of the font (the letters) and use them in bold (fat). A subtitle tells you a bit more about the topic, in one short sentence. The subtitle is usally written in a smaller font, directly under the title.

Graphics:

The graphics you choose, have to make sense with the topic. Choose high resolution graphics, over 300 ppi. If you use a table or a figure, always make sure you use a caption (a title for the figure or table).

TIP: Be careful when browsing the web searching for images. Make sure you stick to the mentioned websites, because sometimes when you download an image, there is a computer virus attached to it and it will infect your computer.

PROJECT:

Whitespace:

This is one of the **most important** aspects of poster design: the space you leave 'empty'. Whitespace means there is no text. This empty space helps create borders around text, helps organize the information is useful blocks and gives the viewer 'breathing space'.

Colors:

Colors draw attention to a poster and also help organize the information. However, using two colors very similar to each other (called low-contrast colors) together makes it very hard to read the information or see the different parts. Using too many colors will make the poster too overwhelming. Try to stick to no more than three colors and try to make these colors complementary (opposite colors on the color wheel, see in the back for a color wheel).

Every color calls for a specific emotion. Blue is often considered calming, green is fresh, red is vibrant, yellow is happy etc. The colors you use should match your topic. If your poster is telling us about a war, the colors you could use would be black, grey, brown, with some red for example.

Using colors to make certain important things pop is a very clever way of adding color to your poster.

TIP: In order to create a sense that all the parts of the poster fit together, you can use colors similar to the colors in graphics. In order to make something stand out, use a complementary color.

PROJECT:

FIRST FARMERS

FARMING STARTED IN THE FERTILE CRESCENT

Let's have a look at our poster again.

What are the colors in this poster, other than black and white?

Beige, sand color, brown, and a bit of green. Canva helps you choose colors that match any images, because they automatically list the colors for each image you use.

What kind of feelings do the colors in this graphic bring? What pops in this poster?

TIP: when making a poster, make different versions of the same poster: try out different lay-outs, different colors. Save each version and when you have a few, look at them again. Usually, you will like one of the designs more than the others.

Your Project:
The Stories of Hud & Saleh (as) have many different elements. Pick one event of one of the stories that you liked very much and represent this in your poster. This week, pay special attention to color. Look at the colors in your image/graphic used, and match or complement them. Change the colors in your template. Create three different versions with different colors. Which one works best with the topic of the story?

Requirements: Pick a pre-made template based upon the parts of the poster needed. Add/remove parts as necessary. Title and subtitle should be correct. Image/graphics should match the topic. Whitespace should be used correctly. Colors should be changed: a minimum of three versions with different colors.

MAP:

Trace the map of the area where prophet Hud (as) & Saleh (as) used to live.

Which map would you need? Where can you find this area on the World Wall Map?

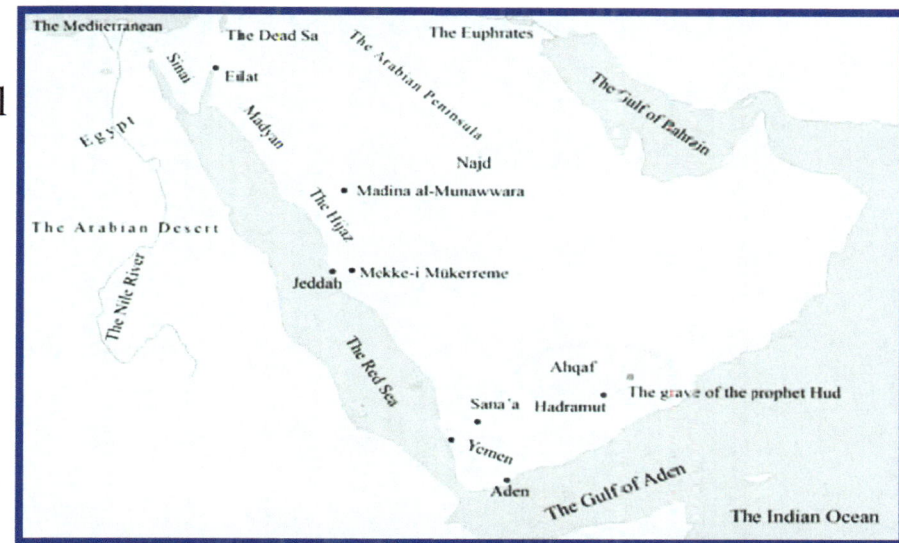

Mark the following:

- Circle and shade the land of Thamud
- Label the land of Thamud
- Circle and shade Ahqaf (people of Hud)
- Label Ahqaf

Use the maps on this page or the maps in the History Intersections, 2nd edition, to help you.

Make sure your map is labeled correctly.

TIMELINE:

Add Prophet Hud (as) and prophet Saleh (as), to your time line. Pay attention to the location: where would you place them?

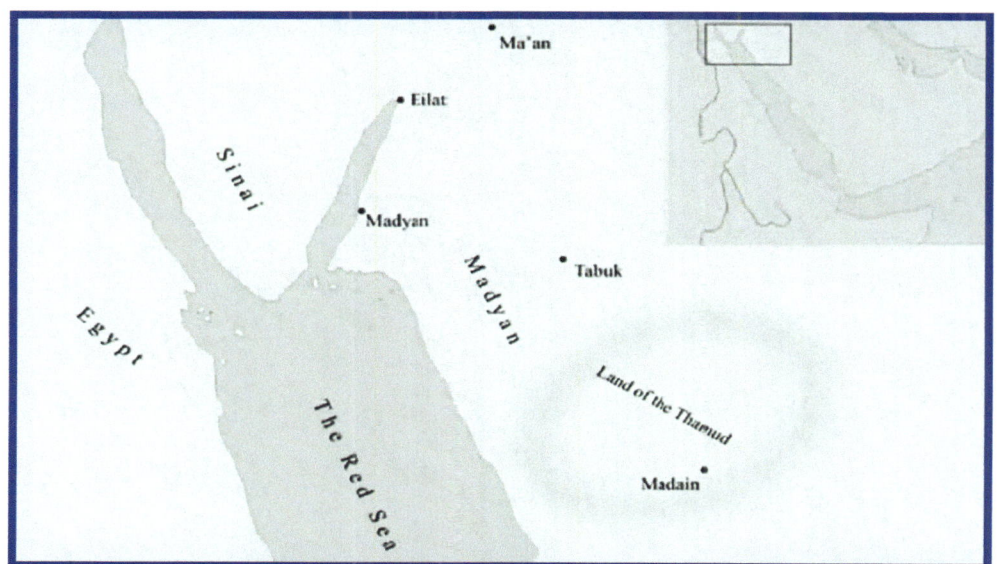

See if you can add any signicant events from this period to your timeline.

WEEK: 6 **PROPHET IBRAHIM (AS) & LUT (AS)**

KEYWORDS: Prophet Ibrahim (as), Prophet Ismail (as), Prophet Ishaq (as), Prophet Lut (as) Nimrod, Makkah

RESOURCES: HI Super Servant Series

SKILL: Outlining

PROJECT: Diagramming

MAPPING: Map of Prophet Ibrahim (as)

TIMELINING: Prophet Ibrahim (as), Prophet Ismail (as)

EXPLANATION

TOPIC: **PROPHET IBRAHIM (AS) & LUT (AS)**

The story of prophet Ibrahim (as) is important to all world religions. We can learn a lot from the way prophet Ibrahim (as) dealt with the disbelievers; he was very intelligent and gentle. Prophet Ibrahim (as) had two sons: Ishaq and Ismail. Both became prophets as well.

Prophet Adam (as) had many sons, and Sheeth (Seth) (as) was the third one. He was also a prophet. Prophet Sheeth (as) was the first one to build the Kaaba. Over time, it broke down with only the foundation remaining. During the flood of prophet Nuh (as), the Kaaba was buried under a thick layer of sand. It remained buried until Prophet Ibrahim (as) and his son prophet Ismail (as) revealed these foundations, and rebuilt the Kaaba.

Lut (as) is the cousin of Prophet Ibrahim (as). He was sent as a prophet to the people of Soddom. They were eventually destroyed due to their horrible disobedience.

RESEARCH:

Day 1:

This week, you will use the History Intersections, 2nd edition.

Remember how to **find information.** Scan the headings and sub-headings in a text to have an idea what the text is talking about.

Ask yourself the questions **before reading**:

- What do I want to learn?
- What do I think the topic is about?

- In which book can I find information?
- What page in this book?
- What are the pages in the book about?

Write down the **difficult words** from the text in your note book, and find the meaning for them.

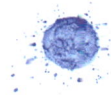

Then ask yourself the questions **during reading** the text:

- What is the writer trying to tell me?
- What is important?
- What happens next?

Ask yourself **after you have read** the text:

- Did I understand what I read?

If you feel you did not understand everything very well, just reread the part you did not understand. Maybe there is a word that you do not know: find the meaning for the word and the text might become clear!

Day 2:
Continue reading your resources. Write down any **difficult words** with their meanings.

Ask yourself the questions **before reading:**

- What do I want to learn?
- What do I think the topic is about?

- In which book can I find information?
- What page in this book?
- What are the pages in the book about?

Then ask yourself the questions **during reading** the text:

- What is the writer trying to tell me?
- What is important?
- What happens next?

Ask yourself these questions **after reading** the text:

- Did I understand what I read?

Now you have gotten the hang of the basic outline, we will go a bit more in detail. We will start to add sub-topics, or details to the main topics. Often, sub-topics include the reason why something happened, when it happened, how it happened, or by whom it happened.

Let us look at the same paragraphs again, and add some details to our outline.

I.   The First people hunted and caught fish

    a.   They did this for thousands of years

II.   Farming started in the Fertile Crescent

    a.   Around 10,000 BCE the weather became better

III.   They planted seeds on purpose

    a.   They saw how seeds fallen grew into new plants

IV.   People began to settle down

    a.   They no longer needed to move around

    b.   They made bricks from mud and clay

Notice how the second level is indented again: moved more to the right than the roman numerals. We often use the lower-case letters of the alphabet to number the sub-topics. You can list as many as needed, but for clarity, we suggest you do not list more than five.

Your Turn:
Outline the topic of this week. For every paragraph, write down one main point, listed with roman numerals. By now, you might think outlining is easy, so add the second level to your outlining this week.

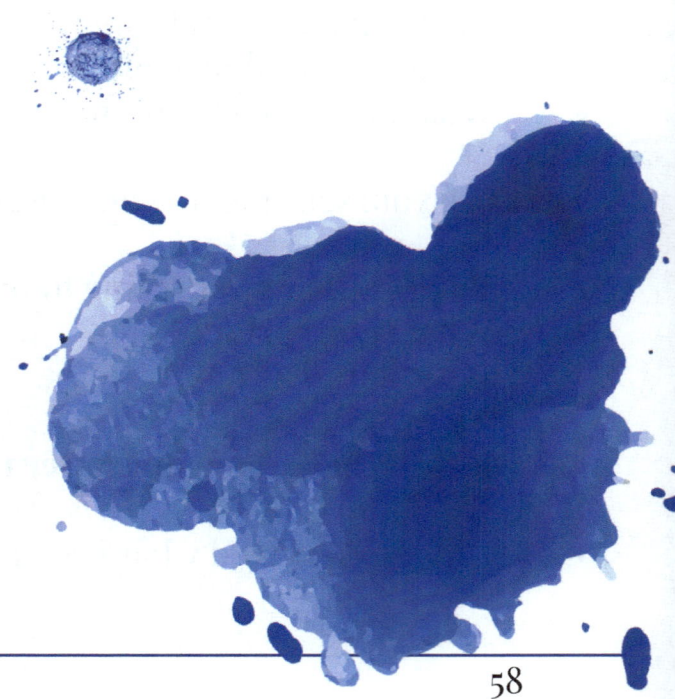

PROJECT: DIAGRAMMING

To diagram means to put information in a visual shape. There are many forms of diagrams. Graph bars, pie charts and sketches are all forms of a diagram.

Using diagrams to show information helps you think about the subject and understand it better. Diagrams help you explore and present ideas. You can simply draw a diagram with a pencil on a paper. You can use different shapes and colors to create a diagram.

Let us have a look at the different examples of diagrams below:

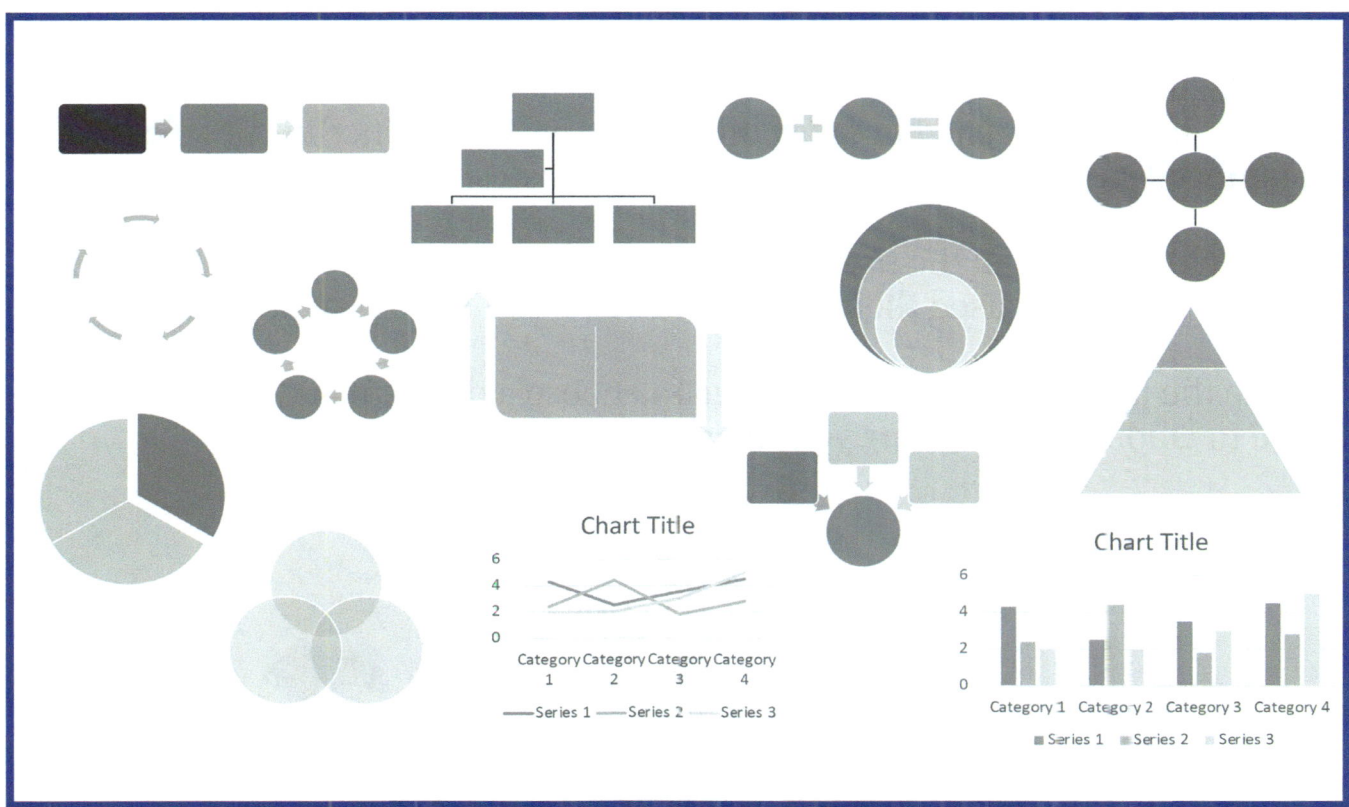

In order to practice making diagrams, we will give you a piece of information you will have to place it in a diagram.

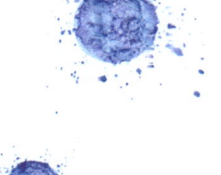

5 Easy Steps to make a diagram:

Step 1: Look at what information you have: how does it relate to each other?
Step 2: Look at the diagrams: what relationship does each diagram show?
Step 3: Choose a diagram that fits your information
Step 4: Draw the diagram
Step 5: Add the information in the diagram

All parts of the diagram need to be labeled. Your drawing does not need to be perfect, but needs to show the problem and your thought process.

Your Turn:

Prophet Ibrahim (as) tried in many different ways to convince his people to remember Allah (swt). Additionally, Allah (swt) also showed them a miracle.

This week, diagram all the times when Ibrahim (as) tried to convince his people, and they could have used their minds and believed in Allah (swt).

Use the the image on the previous page to choose a diagram and use the 5 steps above to guide you in making your diagram.

MAP:

Trace the map of the area where prophet Ibrahim (as) used to live. You should know the name of this area. Do you remember the name? It is Mesopotamia.

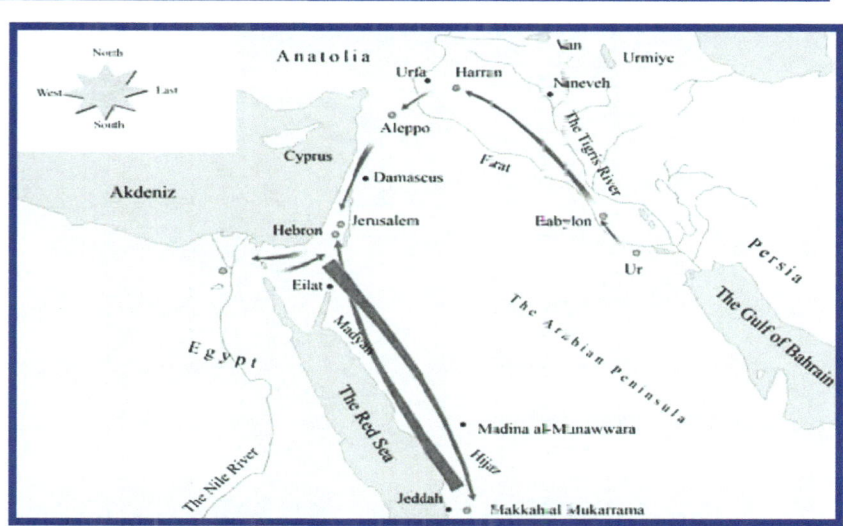

Map the journey of prophet Ibrahim (as). You can use the map on this page, or in the History Intersections, 2nd edition, to help you.

Start by marking off the following:

- Label the rivers, seas and oceans
- Mark Ur
- Mark Harran (in the middle between the ends of the rivers)
- Mark Jerusalem
- Mark Makkah
- Draw an arrow from Ur to Harran
- Draw an arrow from Harran following the coast downward to Jerusalem
- Draw an arrow from Jerusalem to Makkah
- Draw an arrow from Makkah to Jerusalem
- Mark Soddom

Make sure your map is labeled correctly.

TIMELINE:

Add prophet Ibrahim (as), prophet Ismail (as), prophet Ishaq (as) and prophet Lut (as) to your time line. Pay attention to the location: where would you place them?

See if you can add any signicant events from this period to your timeline.

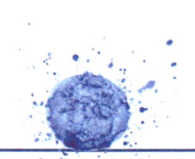

WEEK: 7	**NILE VALLEY**		
KEYWORDS:	Nile, Flooding, Upper Egypt. Lower Egypt	**RESOURCES:**	UILE
SKILL:	Outlining	**PROJECT:**	Diagramming
MAPPING:	Map of Nile Delta	**TIMELINING:**	Egypt

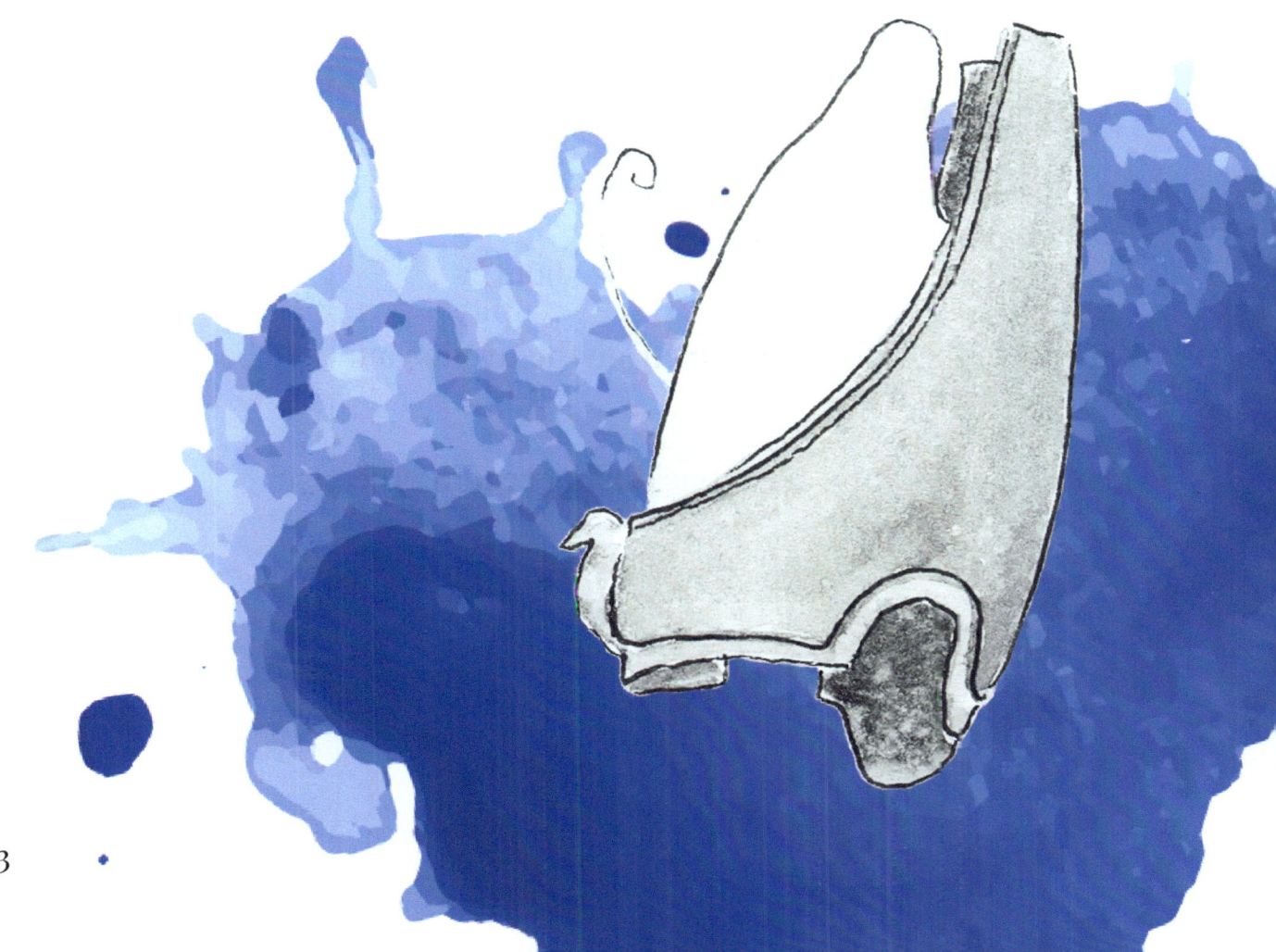

EXPLANATION

TOPIC: NILE VALLEY

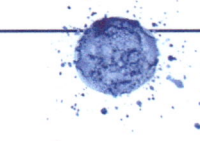

Egypt is almost only desert (90% hot dry desert) BUT it is green and fertile next to the Nile river. Nile means 'neilos' in Greek, which means valley. The Nile is the longest river in the world!

RESEARCH:

Day 1:

This week, you will use the encyclopedia.

Remember how to **find information**. Scan the headings and sub-headings in a text to have an idea what the text is talking about.

Ask yourself the questions **before reading:**

- What do I want to learn?
- What do I think the topic is about?

- In which book can I find information?
- What page in this book?
- What are the pages in the book about?

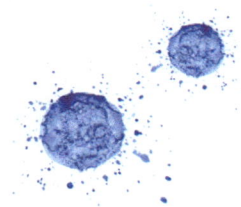

Write down the **difficult words** from the text in your note book, and find the meaning for them.

Then ask yourself the questions **during reading** the text:

- What is the writer trying to tell me?
- What is important?
- What happens next?

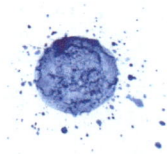

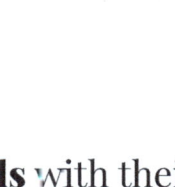

Ask yourself these questions **after reading** the text:

- Did I understand what I read?

Day 2:

Continue reading your resources. Write down any **difficult words** with their meanings.

Ask yourself the questions **before reading:**

- What do I want to learn?
- What do I think the topic is about?

- In which book can I find information?
- What page in this book?
- What are the pages in the book about?

Then ask yourself the questions **during reading** the text:

- What is the writer trying to tell me?
- What is important?
- What happens next?

Ask yourself these questions **after reading** the text:

- Did I understand what I read?

Now you have gotten the hang of the basic outline, we will go a bit more in detail. We will start to add sub-topics, or details to the main topics. Often, sub-topics include the reason why something happened, when it happened, how it happened, or by whom it happened.

Let us look at the same paragraphs again, and add some details to our outline.

I.   The First people hunted and caught fish

    a.   They did this for thousands of years

II.   Farming started in the Fertile Crescent

    a.   Around 10,000 bc the weather became better

III.   They planted seeds on purpose

    a.   They saw how seeds fallen grew into new plants

IV.   People began to settle down

    a.   They no longer needed to move around

    b.   They made bricks from mud and clay

Notice how the second level is indented again: moved more to the right than the roman numerals. We often use the lower-case letters of the alphabet to number the sub-topics. You can list as many as needed, but for clarity, we suggest you do not list more than five.

Your Turn:
Outline the topic of this week. For every paragraph, write down one main point, listed with roman numerals. By now, you might think outlining is easy, so add the second level to your outlining this week.

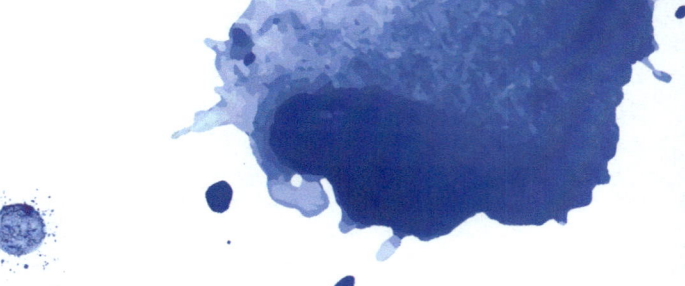

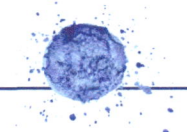

To diagram means to put information in a visual shape. There are many forms of diagrams. Graph bars, pie charts and sketches are all forms of a diagram.

Using diagrams to show information helps you think about the subject and understand it better. Diagrams help you explore and present ideas. You can simply draw a diagram with a pencil on a paper. You can use different shapes and colors to create a diagram.

Let us have a look at the different examples of diagrams below:

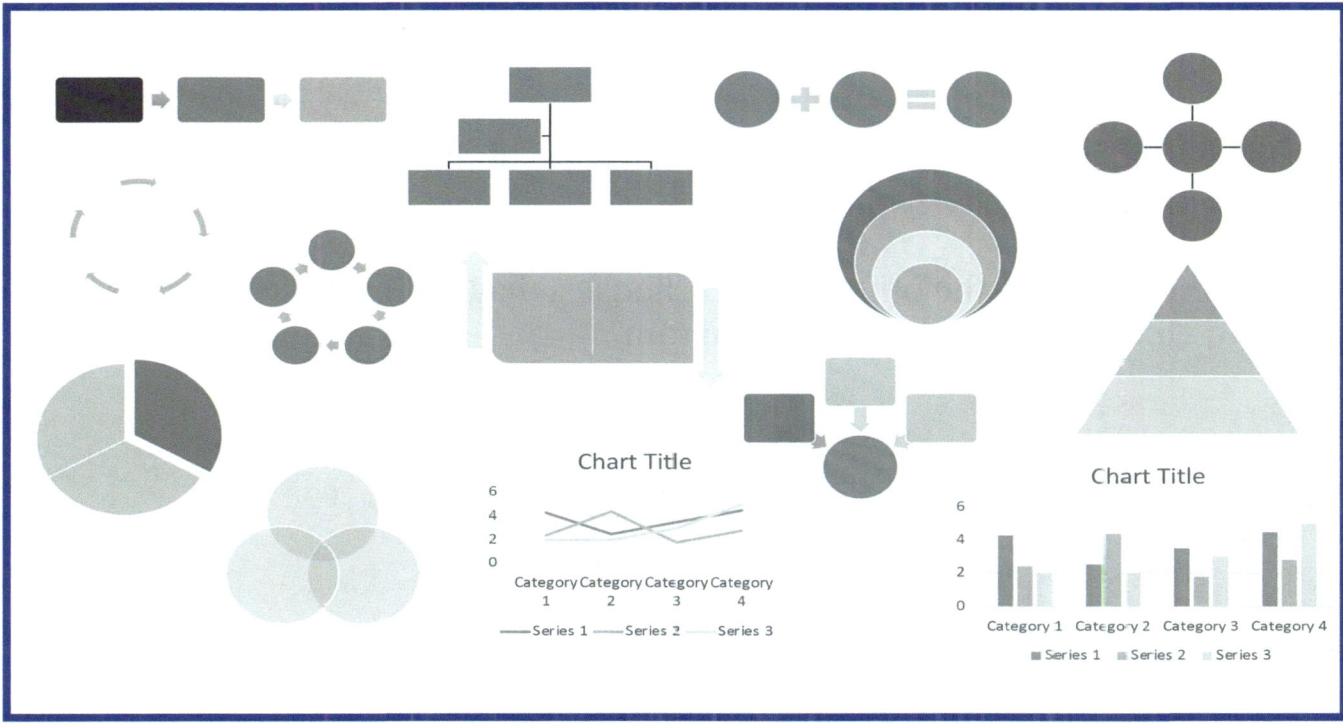

In order to practice making diagrams, we will give you a piece of information you will have to place it in a diagram.

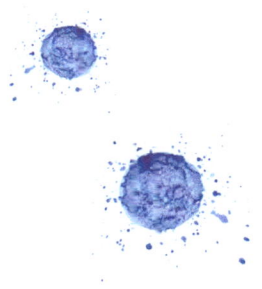

5 Easy Steps to make a diagram:

Step 1: Look at what information you have: how does it relate to each other?
Step 2: Look at the diagrams: what relationship does each diagram show?
Step 3: Choose a diagram that fits your information
Step 4: Draw the diagram
Step 5: Add the information in the diagram

All parts of the diagram need to be labeled. Your drawing does not need to be perfect, but needs to show the problem and your thought process.

Your Turn:

For this week, make a diagram showing the cycle of the Nile, that determined the lives of the ancient Egyptians.

Use the the image on the other page to choose a diagram and use the 5 steps above to guide you in making your diagram.

MAP:

Trace a map of the Nile Delta. Where on the World Wall Map can you find Egypt? Which map will you need to trace?

Mark the following:

- The Nile River and its delta
- The oceans and seas
- Upper Egypt
- Lower Egypt

Use the map in the encyclopedia to help you mark these on your map.

Make sure your map is labeled correctly.

TIMELINE:

Add the union of Upper and Lower Egypt to your timeline. Remember to pay attention to location.

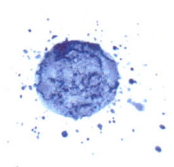

WEEK: 8	EGYPT'S KINGDOMS		
KEYWORDS:	Old, Middle and New Kingdom, Mummies, Pyramids	RESOURCES:	UILE
SKILL:	Note Taking	PROJECT:	Diagramming
MAPPING:	Pyramids of Egypt	TIMELINING:	Old, Middle and New Kingdom

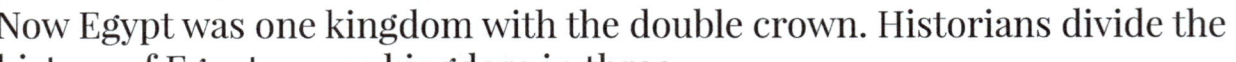

EXPLANATION

TOPIC: EGYPT'S KINGDOMS

Now Egypt was one kingdom with the double crown. Historians divide the history of Egypt as one kingdom in three periods: Old Kingdom, Middle Kingdom and New Kingdom. Egypt is famous for their pyramids and mummies.

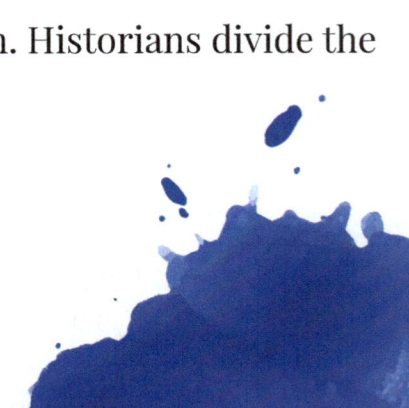

RESEARCH:

Day 1:

This week, you will use the encyclopedia.

Remember how to **find information.** Scan the headings and sub-headings in the text to have an idea what the text is talking about.

Ask yourself the questions **before reading:**

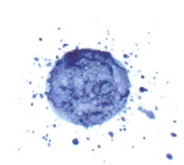

- What do I want to learn?
- What do I think the topic is about?

- In which book can I find information?
- What page in this book?
- What are the pages in the book about?

Write down the **difficult words** from the text in your note book, and find the meaning for them.

Then ask yourself the questions **during reading** the text:

- What is the writer trying to tell me?
- What is important?
- What happens next?

RESEARCH:

Ask yourself these questions **after reading** the text:

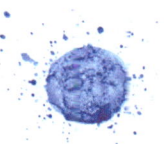

- Did I understand what I read?

Day 2:

Continue reading your resources. Write down any **difficult words** with their meanings.

Ask yourself the questions **before reading:**

- What do I want to learn?
- What do I think the topic is about?

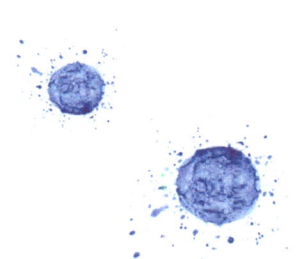

- In which book can I find information?
- What page in this book?
- What are the pages in the book about?

Then ask yourself the questions **during reading** the text:

- What is the writer trying to tell me?
- What is important?
- What happens next?

Ask yourself these questions **after reading** the text:

- Did I understand what I read?

Now, when we are reading a scientific text this way, we need to **check in with ourselves** now and then.

You do this by asking the following questions:

- Am I rereading a part when I do not understand it?
- Am I finding difficult words?

This check-in helps us stay on track. Simply take a few seconds after you have read a page and check in with yourself.

SKILL: NOTE TAKING

Note taking helps you focus on what you are reading, and helps you understand the text better. Good note-taking will help in active listening (if you are taking notes during a lecture for example), understanding and remembrance of the information: it will help you better remember what you read or heard. Making good notes is very important for review and studying for exams. They will save you time and confusion when trying to study a particular topic. Knowing how to make good notes is a skill that will benefit you for your entire life!

What note taking is **NOT:**
- You do not use complete sentences.
- You do not copy sentences from the source.
- You do not use details or examples, unless necessary
- You do not write paragraphs

What note taking **IS:**
- You use phrases and key words
- You use abbreviations
- You use lists and bullet points

Notes do not have to look pretty: they have to be useful. So feel free to use a million arrows, scratch out stuff, or scribble things in between the lines. As long as you can make sense out of the notes and you understand the concept, your notes are great. You are not trying to frame the notes and hang them on your wall: notes are to increase understanding, and as long as they do that, they are perfect, even if they don't look pretty.

Use a specific place where you write down your notes. Loose sheets will not help you much if you lose them or cannot figure out the order of the pages anymore. If you use loose sheets, make it a habit to file them in a binder right away, and make sure you write the date and number the pages from that date. Using different notebooks or separate sections inside one notebook is a simple and effective way to keep your notes organized by subject.

Take your page for note taking and **divide it into two columns:** the left column is only 5 cm wide, and the right column is the rest of the width of the page. In the right column you write down your notes. After you write down your notes, you go over them again and you write in the left column the keywords for the topic and questions you may have.

You can also jot down any questions you have while reading, or anything that is not clear.

Day 1 & 2:

Making notes means just that: you jot down notes. Make sure you still understand your notes afterwards, so find a way to write things down in a short way, but not so short, you will not remember what it meant!

Use your own words for writing down your notes. Only write down what you understand from the text. Make sure you never copy parts from a text that you do not understand: when you go back later to your notes you will certainly not be able to make sense out of it again. The point of note taking is understanding the text.

Keep your notes brief and to the point. Ask yourself: is this essential information or unnecessary? You can use the questions before, during and after reading to help you write down the important points.

Your Turn:

As you read, write down important terms and key words. Leave space next to the terms to add definitions later, if you cannot do so right away. Remember to use your own words!

To diagram means to put information in a visual shape. There are many forms of diagrams. Graph bars, pie charts and sketches are all forms of a diagram.

Using diagrams to show information helps you think about the subject and understand it better. Diagrams help you explore and present ideas. You can simply draw a diagram with a pencil on a paper. You can use different shapes and colors to create a diagram.

Let us have a look at the different examples of diagrams below:

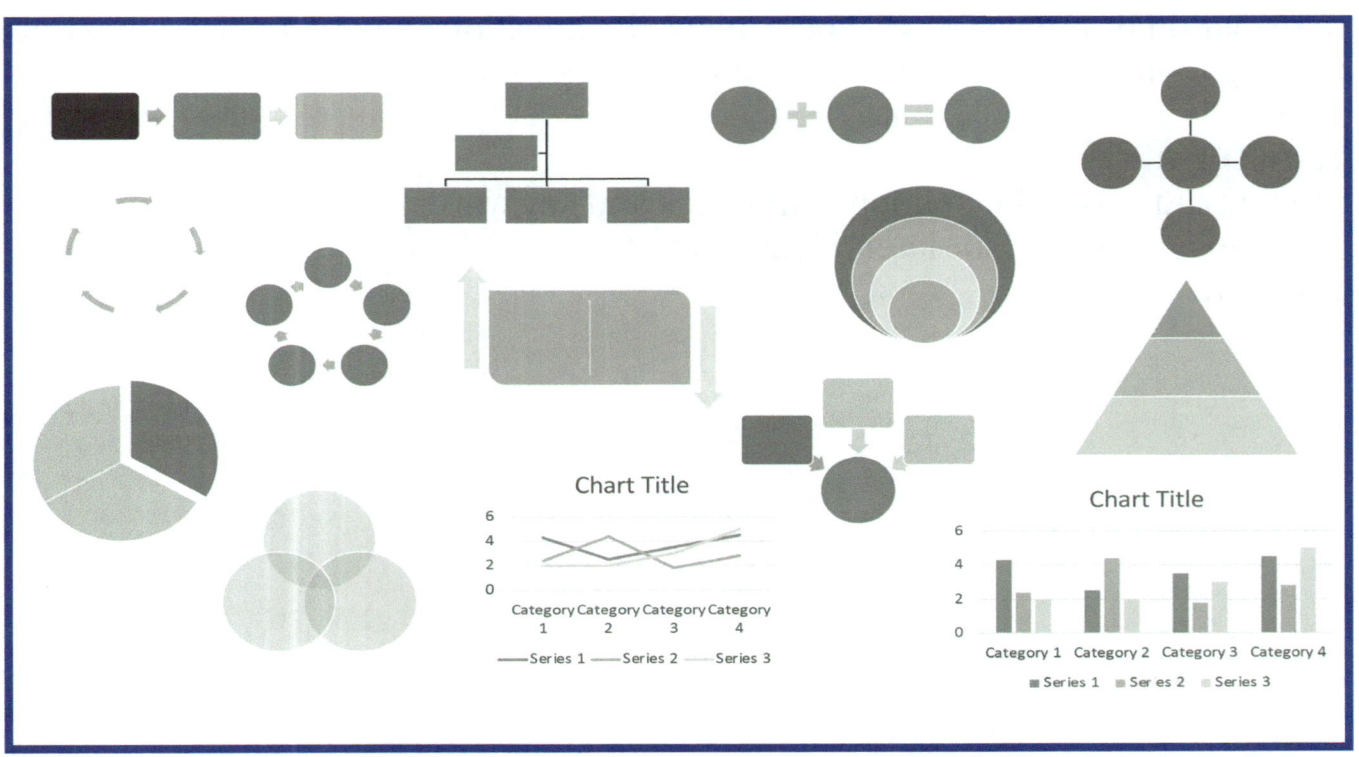

In order to practice making diagrams, we will give you a piece of information you will have to place it in a diagram.

5 Easy Steps to make a diagram:

Step 1: Look at what information you have: how does it relate to each other?
Step 2: Look at the diagrams: what relationship does each diagram show?
Step 3: Choose a diagram that fits your information
Step 4: Draw the diagram
Step 5: Add the information in the diagram

All parts of the diagram need to be labeled. Your drawing does not need to be perfect, but needs to show the problem and your thought process.

Your Turn:

For this week, make a diagram showing the steps of making a mummy, according to the ancient Egyptians.

Use the the image on the other page to choose a diagram and use the 5 steps above to guide you
in making your
diagram.

MAP:

Trace a map of Ancient Egypt. Where on the World Wall Map can you find Mesopotamia? Which map will you need to trace?

Mark the following:

- The River Nile and its delta
- Label the Oceans & Seas
- The Pyramids of Giza
- The Sphinx
- The Valley of the Kings
- The Temple of Luxor

Use the map in the encyclopedia and the one on this page, to help you mark these items on your map.

Make sure your map is labeled correctly.

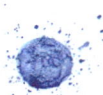

TIMELINE:

Add the Egyptian kingdoms to your timeline.

Use the box with dates in the encyclopedia to add more events to your timeline.

Remember to pay attention to location.

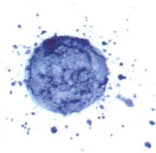

WEEK: 9	**INDUS VALLEY**		
KEYWORDS:	Indus river, Mohenjo-daro, Harappa	**RESOURCES:**	UILE
SKILL:	Note Taking	**PROJECT:**	Diagramming
MAPPING:	Indus Valley	**TIMELINING:**	Indus Valley

EXPLANATION

TOPIC: **INDUS VALLEY**

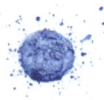

The Indus Valley is one of the ancient civilizations. Many cities thrived next to the Indus river. Two of the biggers cities were called Mohenjo-Daro and Harappa.

RESEARCH:

Day 1 & 2:

This week, you will use the encyclopedia.

Remember how to **find information.** Scan the headings and sub-headings in a text to have an idea what the text is talking about.

Ask yourself the questions **before reading:**

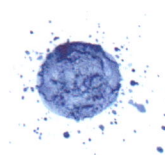

- What do I want to learn?
- What do I think the topic is about?

- In which book can I find information?
- What page in this book?
- What are the pages in the book about?

Write down the **difficult words** from the text in your note book, and find the meaning for them.

Then ask yourself the questions **during reading** the text:

- What is the writer trying to tell me?
- What is important?
- What happens next?

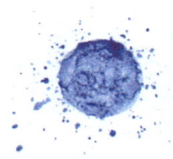

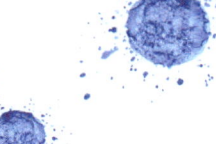

Ask yourself these questions **after reading** the text:

- Did I understand what I read?

Now, when we are reading a scientific text this way, we need to **check in with ourselves** now and then.

You do this by asking the following questions:

- Am I rereading a part when I do not understand it?
- Am I finding difficult words?

This check-in helps us stay on track. Simply take a few seconds after you have read a page and check in with yourself.

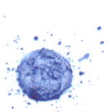

SKILL: NOTE TAKING

Note taking helps you focus on what you are reading, and helps you understand the text better. Good note-taking will help in active listening (if you are taking notes during a lecture for example), understanding and remembrance of the information: it will help you better remember what you read or heard. Making good notes is very important for review and studying for exams. They will save you time and confusion when trying to study a particular topic. Knowing how to make good notes is a skill that will benefit you for your entire life!

What note taking is **NOT:**
- You do not use complete sentences.
- You do not copy sentences from the source.
- You do not use details or examples, unless necessary
- You do not write paragraphs

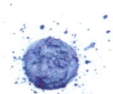

What note taking **IS:**
- You use phrases and key words
- You use abbreviations
- You use lists and bullet points

Notes do not have to look pretty: they have to be useful. So feel free to use a million arrows, scratch out stuff, or scribble things in between the lines. As long as you can make sense out of the notes and you understand the concept, your notes are great. You are not trying to frame the notes and hang them on your wall: notes are to increase understanding, and as long as they do that, they are perfect, even if they don't look pretty.

Use a specific place where you write down your notes. Loose sheets will not help you much if you lose them or cannot figure out the order of the pages anymore. If you use loose sheets, make it a habit to file them in a binder right away, and make sure you write the date and number the pages from that date. Using different notebooks or separate sections inside one notebook is a simple and effective way to keep your notes organized by subject.

Take your page for note taking and **divide it into two columns:** the left column is only 5 cm wide, and the right column is the rest of the width of the page. In the right column you write down your notes. After you write down your notes, you go over them again and you write in the left column the keywords for the topic and questions you may have.

You can also jot down any questions you have while reading, or anything that is not clear.

Day 1 & 2:

Making notes means just that: you jot down notes. Make sure you still understand your notes afterwards, so find a way to write things down in a short way, but not so short, you will not remember what it meant!

Use your own words for writing down your notes. Only write down what you understand from the text. Make sure you never copy parts from a text that you do not understand: when you go back later to your notes you will certainly not be able to make sense out of it again. The point of note taking is understanding the text.

Keep your notes brief and to the point. Ask yourself: is this essential information or unnecessary? You can use the questions before, during and after reading to help you write down the important points.

Your Turn:

As you read, write down important terms and key words. Leave space next to the terms to add definitions later, if you cannot do so right away.
Remember to use your own words!

PROJECT: DIAGRAMMING

To diagram means to out information in a visual shape. There are many forms of diagrams. Graph bars, pie charts and sketches are all forms of a diagram.

Using diagrams to show information helps you think about the subject and understand it better. Diagrams help you explore and present ideas. You can simply draw a diagram with a pencil on a paper. You can use different shapes and colors to create a diagram.

Let us have a look at the different examples of diagrams below:

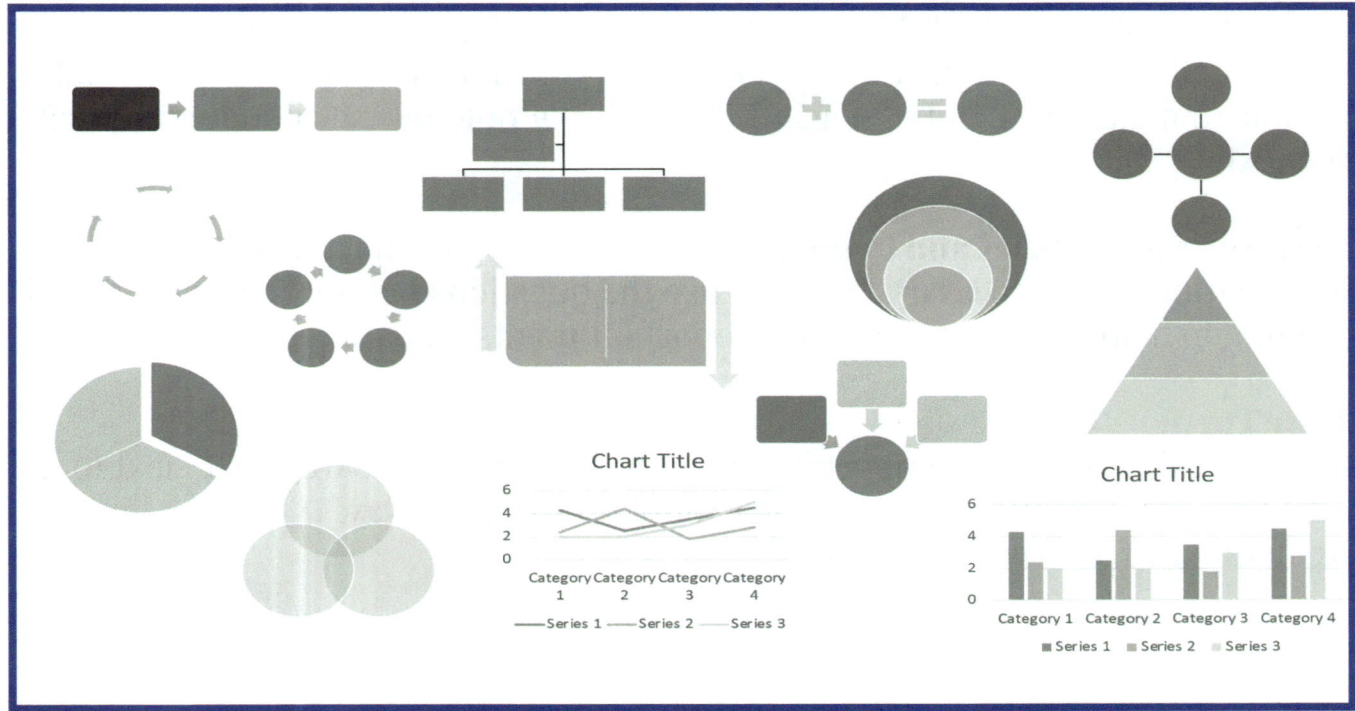

In order to practice making diagrams, we will give you a piece of information you will have to place it in a diagram.

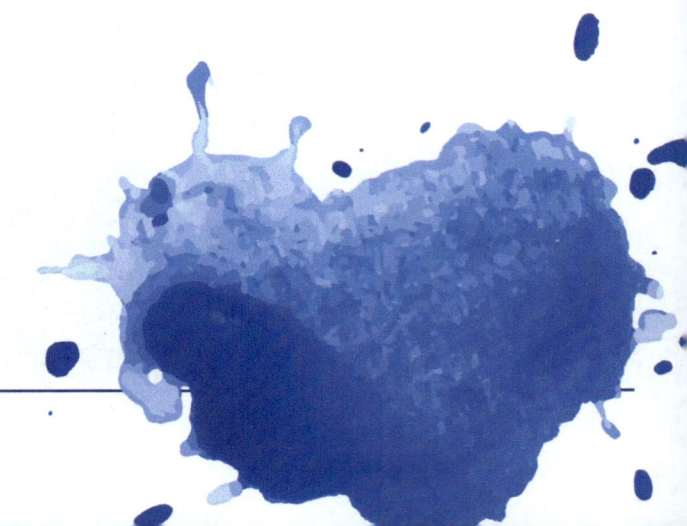

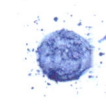

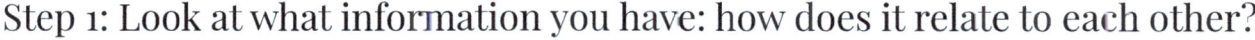

5 Easy Steps to make a diagram:

Step 1: Look at what information you have: how does it relate to each other?
Step 2: Look at the diagrams: what relationship does each diagram show?
Step 3: Choose a diagram that fits your information
Step 4: Draw the diagram
Step 5: Add the information in the diagram

All parts of the diagram need to be labeled. Your drawing does not need to be perfect, but needs to show the problem and your thought process.

Your Turn:

No one has been able to read Indus valley writing. And there is a great mystery in the Indus Valley: Around 1800 BC people started leaving their homes. No one knows why!

Archeologists started to dig in ground around the Indus river. They found remains of a fortress with ruined walls, and some writing but couldn't understand what happened.

Some of the ideas proposed by scientists are:

- A disaster such as a big flood
- Fights between cities
- Grew too much and farmland got ruined
- A disease

For this week, make a diagram showing all the possible reasons why the people of the Indus Valley left their city. See if you can come up with some other reasons why they may have left their cities, and add these to your diagram.

Use the the image on the other page to choose a diagram and use 5 steps above to guide you in making your diagram.

MAP:

Trace a map of the Indus Valley. Where on the World Wall Map can you find the Indus Valley? Which map will you need to trace?

Mark the following:

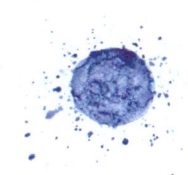

- The River Indus
- Label the Oceans & Seas
- Mohenjo-Daro
- Harappa

Use the map in the encyclopedia to help you mark these items on your map.

Make sure your map is labeled correctly.

TIMELINE:

Add the Indus Valley to your timeline.

Use the box with dates in the encyclopedia to add more events to your timeline.

Remember to pay attention to location.

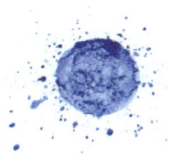

WEEK: 10	PROPHET YA'QUB (AS) & PROPHET YUSUF (AS)		
KEYWORDS:	Prophet Ya'ub (as), Prophet Yusuf (as), Egypt	RESOURCES:	HI Super Servant Series
SKILL:	Note Taking	PROJECT:	Diagramming
MAPPING:	Map of prophet Yusuf (as)	TIMELINING:	Prophet Yusuf (as)

EXPLANATION

TOPIC: **PROPHET YAQ'UB (AS) & PROPHET YUSUF (AS)**

The story of prophet Ya'qub (as) and prophet Yusuf (as)
is related to the story of Prophet
Ibrahim (as).

RESEARCH:

Day 1 & 2:

This week, you will use the History
Intersections, 2nd edition.

Remember how to **find information.** Scan the headings and sub-headings in a
text to have an idea what the text is talking about.

Write down any **difficult words** with their meanings.

Ask yourself the questions **before reading:**

- What do I want to learn?
- What do I think the topic is about?

- In which book can I find information?
- What page in this book?
- What are the pages in the book about?

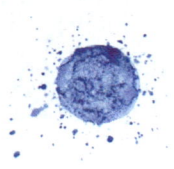

Then ask yourself the questions **during reading** the text:

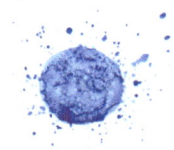

- What is the writer trying to tell me?
- What is important?
- What happens next?

Ask yourself these questions **after reading** the text:

- Did I understand what I read?

Now, when we are reading a scientific text this way, we need to **check in with ourselves** now and then.

You do this by asking the following questions:

- Am I rereading a part when I do not understand it?
- Am I finding difficult words?

This check-in helps us stay on track. Simply take a few seconds after you have read a page and check in with yourself.

The last part of reading a scientific text might very well be the most fun part. Once you have read the text, you should **form your opinion** on the text:

- Do I like what the author said? Why/Why not?
- Are the examples clear? Why/Why not?

Forming an opinion on what you just read helps you understand the text better, especially the 'Why/Why not?' parts. For example, say you just read something about how historians find information. You read the texts, and asked yourself all the questions before, during and after reading. But honestly, you really did not like the text at all! You found it boring, and it had too many difficult words in the text. By knowing you did not like the text, it tells you something about the text as well. Maybe it was written for other historians, and not for kids. Maybe the topic is simply very detailed and confusing, even if someone tries to make it clear, and many other reasons could be mentioned.

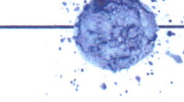

Making good notes is very important for review and studying for exams. They will save you time and confusion when trying to study a particular topic. Knowing how to make good notes is a skill that will benefit you for your entire life!

What note taking is **NOT**:
- You do not use complete sentences.
- You do not copy sentences from the source.
- You do not use details or examples, unless necessary
- You do not write paragraphs

What note taking **IS**:
- You use phrases and key words
- You use abbreviations
- You use lists and bullet points

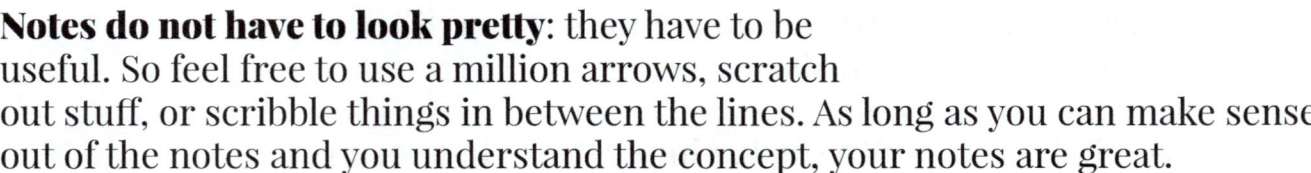

Notes do not have to look pretty: they have to be useful. So feel free to use a million arrows, scratch out stuff, or scribble things in between the lines. As long as you can make sense out of the notes and you understand the concept, your notes are great.

Use a specific place where you write down your notes. Loose sheets will not help you much if you lose them or cannot figure out the order of the pages anymore. If you use loose sheets, make it a habit to file them in a binder right away, and make sure you write the date and number the pages from that date. Using different notebooks or separate sections inside one notebook is a simple and effective way to keep your notes organized by subject.

Take your page for note taking and **divide it into two columns:** the left column is only 5 cm wide, and the right column is the rest of the width of the page. In the right column you write down your notes. After you write down your notes, you go over them again and you write in the left column the keywords for the topic and questions you may have. You can also jot down any questions you have while reading, or anything that is not clear.

Day 1 & 2:

Today, we will start to use **bullet lists and numbered lists.** Use bullet lists for main points. Pay attention to the introduction and conclusion paragraphs, as they often list the main points as well.

Look for key phrases such as "There are four main…" or "To sum up…" or "A major reason why…" Repeated words and concepts are often important ones. Use numbered lists to show sequence or processes. Especially when you see a phrase like "There are four …", use numbers.

Use your own words for writing down your notes. Only write down what you understand from the text. Make sure you never copy parts from a text that you do not understand: when you go back later to your notes you will certainly not be able to make sense out of it again. The point of note taking is understanding the text.

Keep your notes brief and to the point. Ask yourself: is this essential information or unnecessary? You can use the questions before, during and after reading to help you write down the important points.

Your Turn:

As you read, write down important terms and key words. Leave space next to the terms to add definitions later, if you cannot do so right away.

Use at least one list of bullets or numbers in your notes today.

Remember to use your own words!

PROJECT: DIAGRAMMING

5 Easy Steps to make a diagram:

Step 1: Look at what information you have: how does it relate to each other?
Step 2: Look at the diagrams: what relationship does each diagram show?
Step 3: Choose a diagram that fits your information
Step 4: Draw the diagram
Step 5: Add the information in the diagram

All parts of the diagram need to be labeled. Your drawing does not need to be perfect, but needs to show the problem and your thought process.

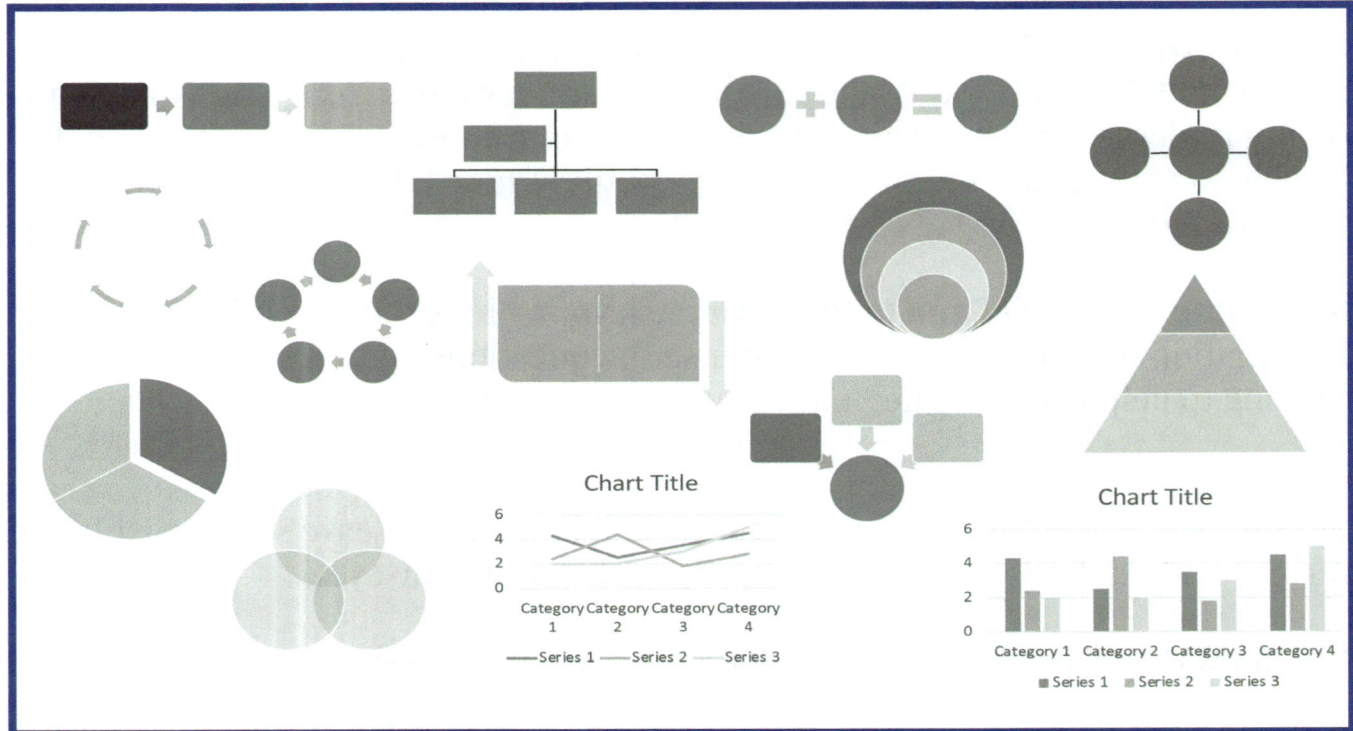

Your Turn:

The stories of the prophets are related to each other through their lineage: their family ties.

For this week, make a diagram showing the lineage of Prophet Ibrahim (as) down to Yusuf (as).

Use the the image on the other page to choose a diagram and use 5 steps above to guide you in making your diagram.

MAP:

Trace the map of the area where prophets Ya'qub (as) and Yusuf (as) used to live. Find the area on the World Wall Map.

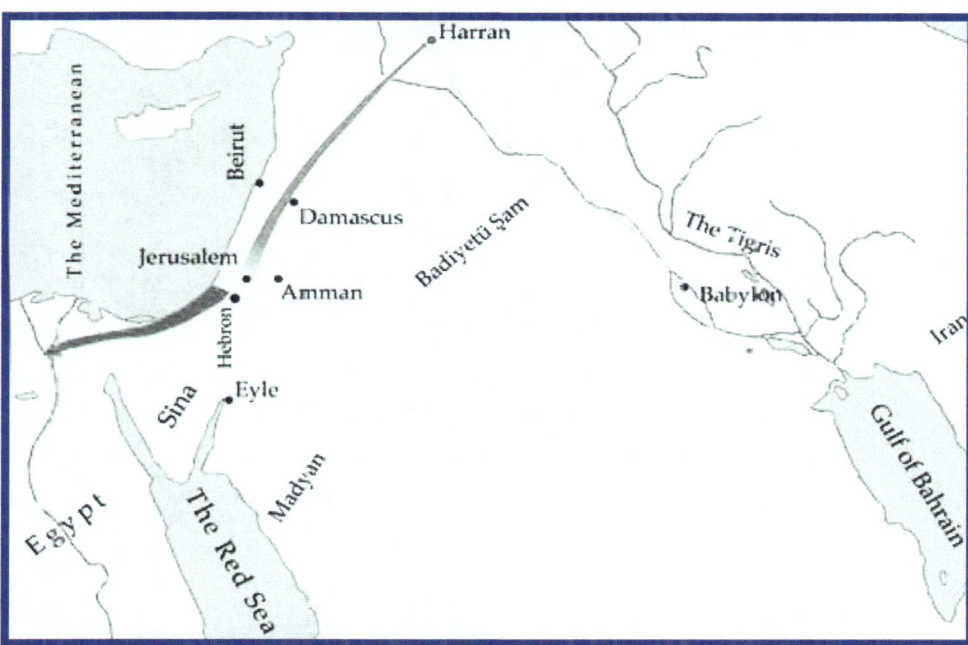

Ya'qub (as) traveled from one area to another area.

He (as) traveled from Mesopotamia to Canaan (Hebron).

Prophet Yusuf (as) was taken from Hebron to Egypt. Map the journey of prophet Ya'qub (as). You can use the map on this page to help you.

Mark the following:

- Label the rivers, seas and oceans
- Mark Harran (in the middle between the ends of the rivers)
- Mark Hebron
- Draw an arrow from Jerusalem to Egypt

Make sure your map is labeled correctly.

TIMELINE:

Add Prophet Ya'qub (as) and prophet Yusuf (as) to your time line. Pay attention to the location: where would you place them?

See if you can add any significant events from this period to your timeline.

WEEK: 11	STONEHENGE & MINOANS		
KEYWORDS:	Stonehenge, King Minos, Knossos, Minotaur	RESOURCES:	UILE
SKILL:	Note taking	PROJECT:	Diagramming
MAPPING:	No map this week	TIMELINING:	Stonehenge & Minoans

EXPLANATION

TOPIC: STONEHENGE & MINOANS

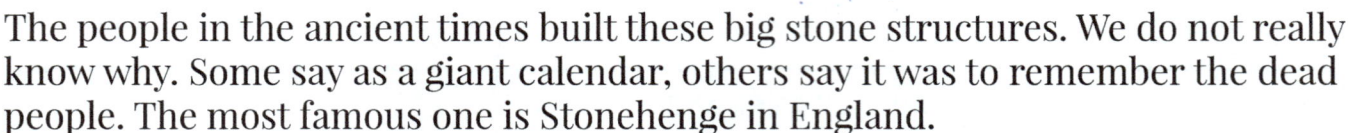

Day 1:

The people in the ancient times built these big stone structures. We do not really know why. Some say as a giant calendar, others say it was to remember the dead people. The most famous one is Stonehenge in England.

Day 2:

In another place in the world, on an island in the Mediterranean Sea called Crete, people were building huge palaces. This was the first civilization of Europe. Remember we spoke about the Indus Valley people, the Fertile Crescent people and the Egyptian Nile Delta?   These were also ancient civilizations but in different areas. And just as in some places people built big temples like the Stonehenge, in Crete they built palaces. The biggest one was the palace of Knossos.

RESEARCH:

Day 1 & 2:

This week, you will use the encyclopedia.

Remember how to **find information.** Scan the headings and sub-headings in a text to have an idea what the text is talking about.

Write down any **difficult words** with their meanings.

Ask yourself the questions **before reading:**

- What do I want to learn?
- What do I think the topic is about?

- In which book can I find information?
- What page in this book?
- What are the pages in the book about?

Then ask yourself the questions **during reading** the text:

*   What is the writer trying to tell me?
*   What is important?
*   What happens next?

Ask yourself these questions **after reading** the text:

*   Did I understand what I read?

Now, when we are reading a scientific text this way, we need to **check in with ourselves** now and then.

You do this by asking the following questions:

*   Am I rereading a part when I do not understand it?
*   Am I finding difficult words?

This check-in helps us stay on track. Simply take a few seconds after you have read a page and check in with yourself.

Once you have read the text, you should **form your opinion** on the text:

*   Do I like what the author said? Why/Why not?
*   Are the examples clear? Why/Why not?

Forming an opinion on what you just read helps you understand the text better, especially the 'Why/Why not?' parts.

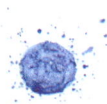

We have started to use **bullet lists and numbered lists.** Use bullet lists for main points. Pay attention to the introduction and conclusion paragraphs, as they often list the main points as well.

Look for key phrases such as "There are four main…" or "To sum up…" or "A major reason why…" Repeated words and concepts are often important ones. Use numbered lists to show sequence or processes. Especially when you see a phrase like "There are four …", use numbers.

Use your own words for writing down your notes. Only write down what you understand from the text. Make sure you never copy parts from a text that you do not understand: when you go back later to your notes you will certainly not be able to make sense out of it again. The point of note taking is understanding the text.

Keep your notes brief and to the point. Ask yourself: is this essential information or unnecessary? You can use the questions before, during and after reading to help you write down the important points.

Your Turn:

As you read, write down important terms and key words. Leave space next to the terms to add definitions later, if you cannot do so right away.

Use at least one list of bullets or numbers in your notes today.

Remember to use your own words!

Read the Story of the Minotaur below:

Legend of the Minotaur

Once upon a time, a long time ago, there lived a king named Minos. King Minos lived on a lovely island called Crete. King Minos had everything a king could possibly want. Now and then, King Minos sent his navy to the tiny village of Athens, across the sea. King Minos only attacked Athens when he was bored. He really didn't want anything.

The king of Athens did not know what to do. He was desperate. He figured if he had some time, he could build a strong navy, strong enough to send King Minos packing the next time he attacked Athens. The king of Athens offered King Minos a deal. If he would not attack Athens for 9 years, Athens would send 7 boys and 7 girls to the island of Crete to be eaten by the awful monster that King Minos kept as a pet, the dreaded Minotaur.

The Minotaur lived in the heart of a maze on the island of Crete. The Minotaur had the head of a bull and the body of a man. King Minos loved that old monster. He took the deal so that his beloved monster could look forward to a special treat every 9 years or so.

Although Athens did build a navy, King Minos did not attack as the king of Athens had expected. In fact, King Minos kept his word. And now it was time for Athens to keep theirs. Everyone in Athens was crying.

Prince Theseus of Athens knew the importance of keeping your word. He knew that a deal was a deal. But, he was also quite sure that it was wrong to send small children to be eaten by a monster. Prince Theseus told his father (the king) that he was going to Crete as the seventh son of Athens. He was going to kill the Minotaur and end the terror.

"The Minotaur is a terrible monster! What makes you think you can kill it?" cried his father.

"I'll find a way," Theseus replied gently. "The gods will help me."

His father begged him not to go. But the prince took his place as the seventh Athenian boy. Along with six other Athenian boys and seven Athenian girls, Prince Theseus sailed towards Crete.

When the prince and the children arrived on the island of Crete, King Minos and his daughter, the Princess Ariadne, came out to greet them. The Princess Ariadne did not say anything. But her eyes narrowed thoughtfully. Late that night, she wrote Prince Theseus a note and slipped it under his bedroom door.

She offered him a deal because she was bored and wanted to leave Crete. She would help Theseus kill the Minotaur and in return, he would take her away from the Island so everyone could admire how beautiful she was. If he was interested, he should meet her by the gate of the Labyrinth.

Princess Ariadne was indeed very beautiful and Theseus could use some help in his quest to kill the monster. So prince Theseus slipped out of the palace and waited patiently by the gate. Princess Ariadne finally showed up. In her hands, she carried a sword and a ball of string.

Princess Ariadne gave the sword and the ball of string to Prince Theseus. "Hide these inside the entrance to the maze. Tomorrow, when you and the other children from Athens enter the Labyrinth, wait until the gate is closed, then tie the string to the door. Unroll it as you move through the maze. That way, you can find your way back again. The sword, well, you know what to do with the sword," she said as she laughed.

Theseus thanked the princess for her kindness. "Don't forget, now," she cautioned Theseus. "You must take me with you so all the people can admire me."

The next morning, the Athenian children, including Prince Theseus, were shoved into the maze. The door was locked firmly behind them. Following Ariadne's directions, Theseus tied one end of the string to the door. He told the children to stay by the door and to make sure the string stayed tied so the prince could find his way back again. The children hung on to the string tightly, as Theseus entered the maze alone.

Deep inside the maze, Theseus heard bone chilling roaring. He was getting close to the monster. All of a sudden the monster appeared, ready to kill Theseus. A heated battle ensued. Using the sword Ariadne had given him, Theseus killed the monstrous beast. He followed the string back and knocked on the door.

Princess Ariadne was waiting. She opened the door. Without anyone noticing, Prince Theseus and the children of Athens ran to their ship and sailed quietly away. Princess Ariadne sailed away with them.

On the way home, they stopped for supplies on the tiny island of Naxos. Princess Ariadne insisted on coming ashore. There was nothing much to do on the island. Soon, she fell asleep. All the people gathered to admire the sleeping princess. Theseus sailed quietly away with the children of Athens and left her there, sleeping. After all, a deal is a deal.

PROJECT:

5 Easy Steps to make a diagram:

Step 1: Look at what information you have: how does it relate to each other?
Step 2: Look at the diagrams: what relationship does each diagram show?
Step 3: Choose a diagram that fits your information
Step 4: Draw the diagram
Step 5: Add the information in the diagram

All parts of the diagram need to be labeled. Your drawing does not need to be perfect, but needs to show the problem and your thought process.

Your Turn:

Diagram the events of the story The Legend of the Minotaur. Show step by step what happened.

Use the the image on the this page to choose a diagram and use 5 steps above to guide you in making your diagram.

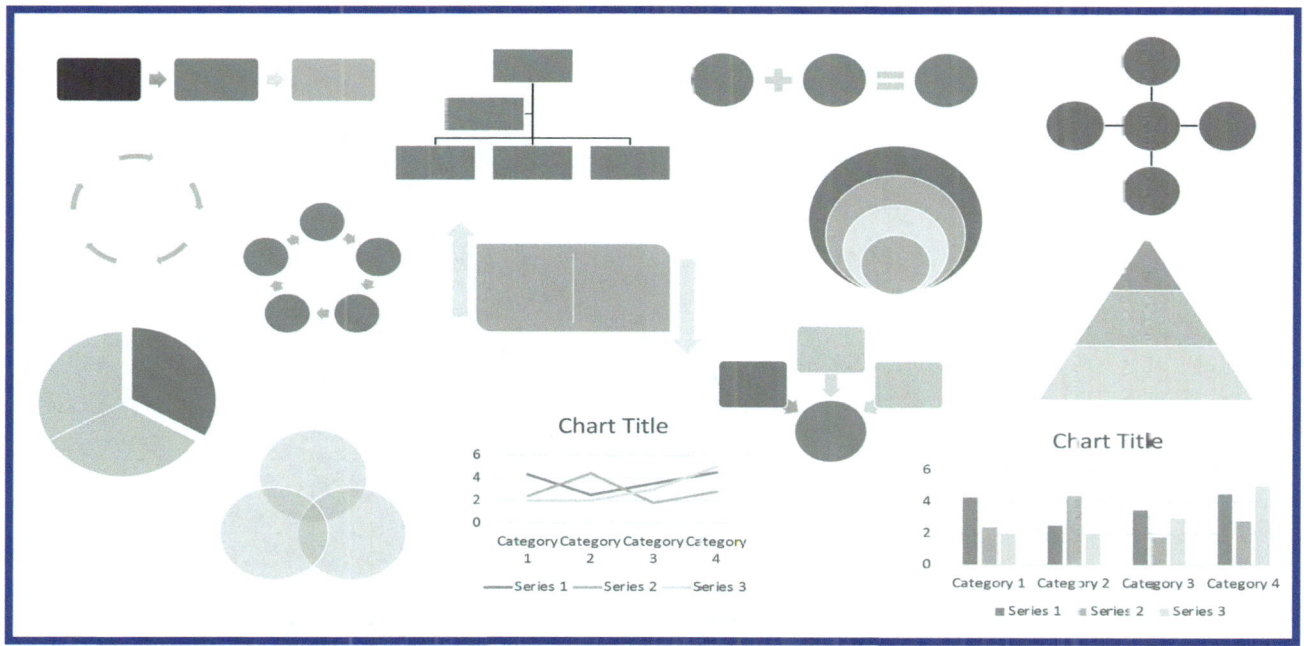

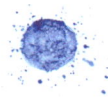

MAP:

There is no map this week! Spend some time organizing the maps you have made so far, in your folder. Go through them and see if any of them are missing labels.

As you glance over them, see if you can remember the information you covered that week.

TIMELINE:

Add Stonehenge and the Minoans to your timeline.

Use the boxes with dates in the encyclopedia to add more events to your timeline.

Remember to pay attention to location.

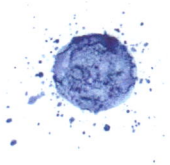

WEEK: 12   **MYCENEANS**

KEYWORDS: Myceneans, Troy   **RESOURCES:**   UILE

SKILL: Note Taking   **PROJECT:**   PowerPoint

MAPPING: Greece   **TIMELINING:**   Mycenea

EXPLANATION

TOPIC: MYCENEANS

Mycenea was a city in ancient Greece. They loved to go to war. They had trained soldiers and fast chariots.

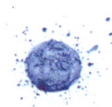

RESEARCH:

Day 1 & 2:
This week, you will use the encyclopedia.

Remember how to **find information.** Scan the headings and sub-headings in a text to have an idea what the text is talking about.

Write down any **difficult words** with their meanings.

Ask yourself the questions **before reading:**

- What do I want to learn?
- What do I think the topic is about?

- In which book can I find information?
- What page in this book?
- What are the pages in the book about?

Then ask yourself the questions **during reading** the text:

- What is the writer trying to tell me?
- What is important?
- What happens next?

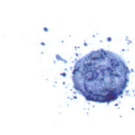
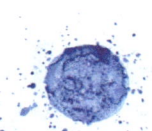

Ask yourself these questions **after reading** the text:

- Did I understand what I read?

Now, when we are reading a scientific text this way, we need to **check in with ourselves** now and then.

You do this by asking the following questions:

- Am I rereading a part when I do not understand it?
- Am I finding difficult words?

This check-in helps us stay on track. Simply take a few seconds after you have read a page and check in with yourself.

Once you have read the text, you should **form your opinion** on the text:

- Do I like what the author said? Why/Why not?
- Are the examples clear? Why/Why not?

Forming an opinion on what you just read helps you understand the text better, especially the 'Why/Why not?' parts.

Day 1 & 2:

We have started to use **bullet lists and numbered lists.** Use bullet lists for main points. Pay attention to the introduction and conclusion paragraphs, as they often list the main points as well.

Look for key phrases such as "There are four main..." or "To sum up..." or "A major reason why..." Repeated words and concepts are often important ones. Use numbered lists to show sequence or processes. Especially when you see a phrase like "There are four ...", use numbers.

Use your own words for writing down your notes. Only write down what you understand from the text. Make sure you never copy parts from a text that you do not understand: when you go back later to your notes you will certainly not be able to make sense out of it again. The point of note taking is understanding the text.

Keep your notes brief and to the point. Ask yourself: is this essential information or unnecessary? You can use the questions before, during and after reading to help you write down the important points.

Now, we will pay special attention to using **abbreviations**.

Abbreviations are used in place of words that come in a text very frequently, but are important for understanding. For example, the word 'because' is important, as it shows you what came before.

When you abbreviate, use the first part of the word. So 'because' can become 'bec.'. You can also use the first part and the last letter of a word to make an abbreviation, like 'gov't' for government.

Another way is to leave out the vowels: we are very capable of reading words without vowels. Try the following words: prblm, or schl. Did you figure it out? They were problem and school.

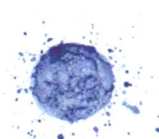

You can make up your own abbreviations, as long as you remember later on what they stand for! When you read today, try to come up with at least one abbreviation.

Your Turn:
As you read, write down important terms and key words. Leave space next to the terms to add definitions later, if you cannot do so right away.

Use bullet lists and number lists when useful. Come up with at least one abbreviation in your notes today.

Remember to use your own words!

PROJECT: POWERPOINT

A PowerPoint presentation is often used in combination with a lecture or speech. It is used as a visual support of what you are saying, so it never contains every single word of your speech.
As you make a speech or lecture, the slides should move along. Whatever is on the slides, is included in what you say. Slides show the information in simplified form.

Microsoft PowerPoint is one of the most used program on Windows computers. On Apple computers, you can use Keynote, which is a similar program.

When we mention PPT, it means your PowerPoint presentation, regardless of the software you use.

Steps for good PPT presentations:

Step 1: Research your topic
Step 2: Make a quick outline
Step 3: Choose a template
Step 4: One main point per slide
Step 5: Keep the design simple

This week, we will focus on steps 1 & 2:

Step 1: Research your topic. The easiest way is to make note of the main points of the topic. Ask yourself the research questions to extract the most important information

Step 2: Write a quick outline on what your PPT is about. Think of who you are writing this presentation for: who is your audience?

Make sure you list the main points. Slides should never contain full paragraphs. Use your own words: do not copy/paste from a text.

Make an introduction. In the introduction you introduce the topic sentence (or thesis) and give a summary of your PPT. A topic sentence is a statement that captures what your PPT is about. The introduction is supposed to make the audience curious about your presentation.

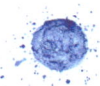

PROJECT:

Create a **conclusion sentence:** restate the topic sentence (or thesis) and add a call to action, or a bold statement. The conclusion is supposed to make your audience feel they got something out of your presentation.

Your Turn:

You have already researched your topic for this week, so write a quick outline about the main events. Think of a catchy title and a topic sentence.

Create a PPT with a minimum of **5 slides:** one introduction slide, 3 main point slides (one main point per slide) and one conclusion slide.

The design can be simply a colored background: we will pay more attention to the design in later weeks.

MAP:

Trace the map of Greece. Which map do you need? Where can you find this area on the World Wall Map?

Mark the following:
- Mark the seas & oceans
- Mark Athens
- Mark Crete
- Mark Knossos
- Mark Mycenea
- Mark Troy
- Draw an arrow from Athens to Knossos
- Draw an arrow, with a different color, from Mycenea to Troy

Look at the maps in the encyclopedia for help.

Make sure your map is labeled correctly.

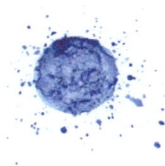

TIMELINE:

Add the Myceneans to your timeline.

Use the box with dates in the encyclopedia to add more events to your timeline.

Remember to pay attention to location.

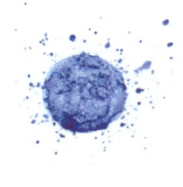

WEEK: 13	**PROPHET AYYUB (AS) & DHUL KIFL (AS)**		
KEYWORDS:	Prophet Ayyub (as), Dhul Kifl (as)	**RESOURCES:**	HI Super Servants Series
SKILL:	Note Taking	**PROJECT:**	PowerPoint
MAPPING:	Prophet Ayyub (as), Dhul Kifl (as)	**TIMELINING:**	Prophet Ayyub (as), Dhul Kifl (as)

EXPLANATION

TOPIC: PROPHET AYYUB (AS) & DHUL KIFL (AS)

Prophet Ayyub (as) had to bear many losses and he suffered a lot. He could deal with all these trials, because he felt intensely grateful for all the blessings he had been given.

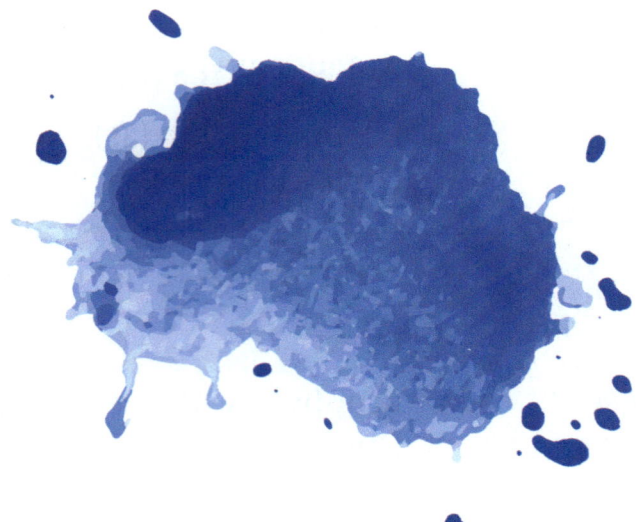

Dhul Kifl (as) was the son of Ayyub (as) who received prophethood as well.

RESEARCH:

Day 1 & 2:
You now know exactly what to do,
in order to read a text properly. Every week you will find and read the resources for your topic, and ask yourself these questions. We have provided you with a **cheat sheet**, that helps you remember the questions.

Below is a **short check-list:**

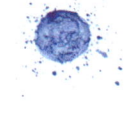

* Find your resources
* Ask yourself the questions before reading
* Write down difficult words
* Read the text
* Ask yourself the questions during reading
* Ask yourself the questions after reading
* Check in with yourself
* Form your opinion

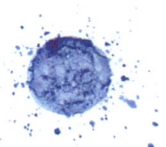

TIP: Take the cheat sheet out of the book and keep it next to you when you read and make notes.

Day 1 & 2:

We have started to use **bullet lists and numbered lists.** Use bullet lists for main points. Pay attention to the introduction and conclusion paragraphs, as they often list the main points as well.

Look for key phrases such as "There are four main…" or "To sum up…" or "A major reason why…" Repeated words and concepts are often important ones. Use numbered lists to show sequence or processes. Especially when you see a phrase like "There are four …", use numbers.

Use your own words for writing down your notes. Only write down what you understand from the text. Make sure you never copy parts from a text that you do not understand: when you go back later to your notes you will certainly not be able to make sense out of it again. The point of note taking is understanding the text.

Keep your notes brief and to the point. Ask yourself: is this essential information or unnecessary? You can use the questions before, during and after reading to help you write down the important points.

Today, we will pay special attention to using **abbreviations**.

Abbreviations are used in place of words that come in a text very frequently, but are important for understanding. For example, the word 'because' is important, as it shows you what came before.

When you abbreviate, use the first part of the word. So 'because' can become 'bec.'. You can also use the first part and the last letter of a word to make an abbreviation, like 'gov't' for government.

Another way is to leave out the vowels: we are very capable of reading words without vowels. Try the following words: prblm, or schl. Did you figure it out? They were problem and school.

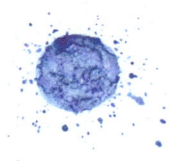

SKILL:

You can make up your own abbreviations, as long as you remember later on what they stand for! When you read today, try to come up with at least one abbreviation.

Your Turn:

As you read, write down important terms and key words. Leave space next to the terms to add definitions later, if you cannot do so right away.

Use bullet lists and number lists when useful. Come up with at least *two more* abbreviations in your notes today.

Remember to use your own words!

PROJECT: POWERPOINT

A PowerPoint presentation is often used in combination with a lecture or speech. It is used as a visual support of what you are saying, so it never contains every single word of your speech. As you make a speech or lecture, the slides should move along. Whatever is on the slides, is included in what you say. Slides show the information in simplified form.

Microsoft PowerPoint is the most used program on Windows computers. On Apple computers, you can use Keynote, which is a similar program.

When we mention PPT, it means your PowerPoint presentation, regardless of the software you use.

Steps for good PPT presentations:

Step 1: Research your topic
Step 2: Make a quick outline
Step 3: Choose a template
Step 4: One main point per slide
Step 5: Keep the design simple

This week, we will focus on steps 1,2 & 3:

Step 1: Research your topic. The easiest way is to make note of the main points of the topic. Ask yourself the research questions to extract the most important information

Step 2: Write a quick outline on what your PPT is about. Think of who you are writing this presentation for: who is your audience?

Make sure you list the main points. Slides should never contain full paragraphs. Use your own words: do not copy/paste from a text.

Make an introduction. In the introduction you introduce the topic sentence (or thesis) and give a summary of your PPT. A topic sentence is a statement that captures what your PPT is about. The introduction is supposed to make the audience curious about your presentation.

PROJECT:

Create a conclusion sentence: restate the topic sentence (or thesis) and add a call to action, or a bold statement. The conclusion is supposed to make your audience feel they got something out of your presentation.

Step 3: Choose a template. There are many template but try to choose one that fits your topic. A slide template can have different lay-outs. Titles can be at the top, left side or right side. There can be space for a graphic (a graph or an image).

Your Turn:

You have already researched your topic for this week, so write a quick outline about the main events. Think of a catchy title and a topic sentence.

Pick a template to use for your presentation this week.

Create a PPT with a minimum of 5 slides: one introduction slide, 3 main point slides (one main point per slide) and one conclusion slide.

Map of Ayyub (as)

Trace the map for the area where the prophets used to live. Which map would you need? Where is this area located on the World Wall Map?

Mark the following in your map:
- Label the seas and oceans
- Mark Damascus
- Shade the area where prophet Ayyub (as) resided.

You can look at the map on this page for help.

Make sure your map is labeled correctly.

TIMELINE:

Add Prophet Ayyub (as) and Dhul Kifl (as) to your time line. Pay attention to the location: where would you place them?

See if you can add any significant events from this period to your timeline.

WEEK: 14	**HAMMURABI & THE HITTITES**		
KEYWORDS:	Hammurabi's Law, Babylonian Empire, Hittites	**RESOURCES:**	UILE
SKILL:	Note Taking	**PROJECT:**	PowerPoint
MAPPING:	Babylonian Empire & the Hittite Empire	**TIMELINING:**	Babylonian Empire & the Hittite Empire

EXPLANATION

TOPIC:

We learned that both prophet Ibrahim (as) and Nuh (as) lived in the the Fertile Crescent. We also learned about Sumer, Akkad and King Argon. After a while new tribes began to settle in the lands of Sumer and Akkad. Each city became its own kingdom. But then one day, a young man called Hammurabi became king of the city of Babylon. Hammurabi fought with all the other cities and won. Now they were all together in one empire under king Hammurabi.

No matter how strong Hammurabi's empire was, eventually, all empires will end. Usually they end because another, stronger empire invades them. In the case of Hammurabi's empire, these were the Hittites. The Hittites sort of lived next door and they were tough warriors, and they had chariots! Do you remember who else had chariots? Yes, the Mycenaeans and they loved war as well. The Hittites not only had chariots, they also had iron weapons.

RESEARCH:

Day 1 & 2:

You know what to do!

Find your resources, and read the text. Use the check-list below and the **cheat sheet** to ask yourself the questions.

Check-list:

- Find your resources
- Ask yourself the questions before reading
- Write down difficult words
- Read the text
- Ask yourself the questions during reading
- Ask yourself the questions after reading
- Check in with yourself
- Form your opinion

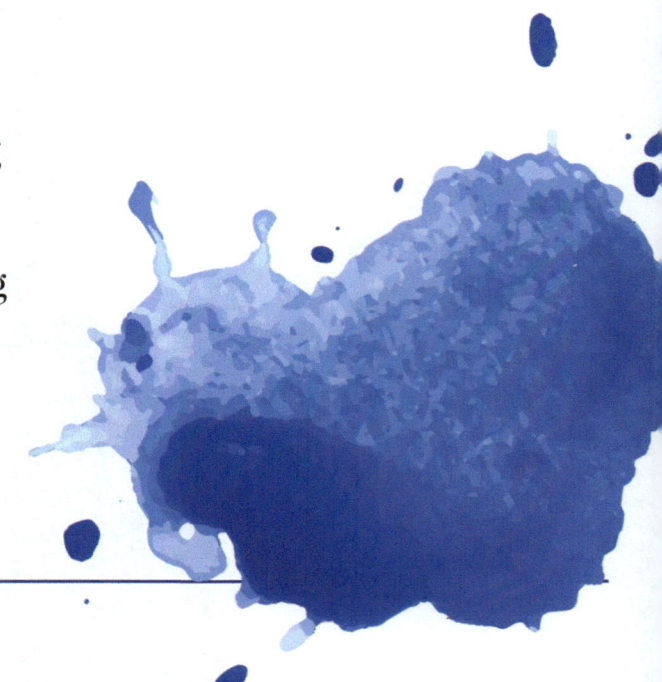

Day 1 & 2:

Use your own words for writing down your notes. Only write down what you understand from the text. Make sure you never copy parts from a text that you do not understand: when you go back later to your notes, you will certainly not be able to make sense out of it again. The point of note taking is understanding the text.

Keep your notes **brief and to the point**. Ask yourself: is this essential information or unnecessary? You can use the questions before, during and after reading to help you write down the important points.

Use **bullet lists** for main points. Pay attention to the introduction and conclusion paragraphs, as they often list the main points as well. Look for key phrases such as "There are four main..." or "To sum up..." or "A major reason why..." Repeated words and concepts are often important ones.

Use **numbered lists** to show sequence or processes. Especially when you see a phrase like "There are four ...", use numbers.

We have started to pay special attention to using **abbreviations**.

Abbreviations are used in place of words that come in a text very frequently, but are important for understanding. For example, the word 'because' is important, as it shows you what came before.

When you abbreviate, use the first part of the word. So 'because' can become 'bec.'.

You can also use the first part and the last letter of a word to make an abbreviation, like 'gov't' for government.

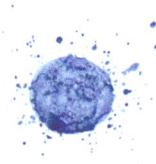

Another way is to leave out the vowels: we are very capable of reading words without vowels. Try the following words: prblm, or schl. Did you figure it out? They were problem and school.

You can make up your own abbreviations, as long as you remember later on what they stand for!

Your Turn:

As you read, write down important terms and key words. Leave space next to the terms to add definitions later, if you cannot do so right away.

Use bullet lists and number lists when useful. Come up with at least *three more* abbreviations in your notes today.

Remember to use your own words!

PROJECT: **POWERPOINT**

Steps for good PPT presentations:

Step 1: Research your topic
Step 2: Make a quick outline
Step 3: Choose a template
Step 4: One main point per slide
Step 5: Keep the design simple

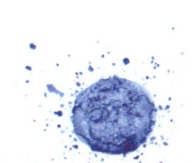

This week, we will focus on steps 1 through 4:

Step 1: Research your topic. The easiest way is to make note of the main points of the topic. Ask yourself the research questions to extract the most important information

Step 2: Write a quick outline on what your PPT is about. Think of who you are writing this presentation for: who is your audience?

Make sure you list the main points. Slides should never contain full paragraphs. Use your own words: do not copy/paste from a text.

Make an introduction. In the introduction you introduce the topic sentence (or thesis) and give a summary of your PPT. Create a conclusion sentence: restate the topic sentence (or thesis) and add a call to action, or a bold statement.

Step 3: Choose a template. There are many template but try to choose one that fits your topic. A slide template can have different lay-outs. Titles can be at the top, left side or right side. There can be space for a graphic (a graph or an image).

Step 4: Use one main point for every slide. Present the information in short sentences or phrases. Use bullet points or numbers to present the information.

Your Turn:

You have already researched your topic for this week, so write a quick outline about the main events. Think of a catchy title and a topic sentence.

Pick a template to use for your presentation this week.

Add at least **one image or clip art** to your presentation that supports the main point.

Create a PPT with a minimum of **5 slides:** one introduction slide, 3 main point slides (one main point per slide) and one conclusion slide.

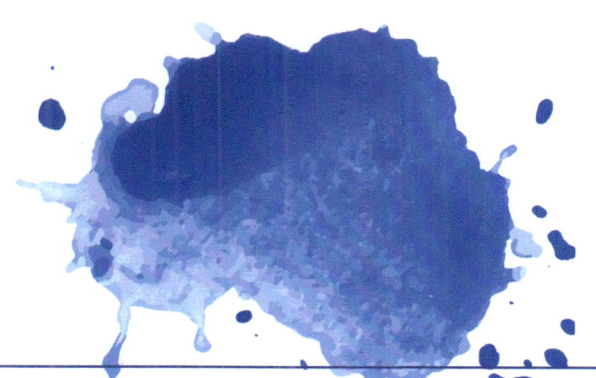

MAP:

Trace the map for the Babylonian & Hittite Empire: which map do you need? Where can you find this area on the World Wall Map?

Mark in your map the following:
- Label the seas & oceans
- Color the rivers blue and label them
- Mark Babylon
- Shade the Babylonian Empire purple
- Mark Hattushash
- Shade the Hittite Empire blue

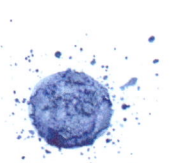

Use the maps in the encyclopedia to help you.

Make sure your map is labeled correctly.

TIMELINE:

Add the Babylonian & Hittite Empire to your timeline.

Use the boxes with dates in the encyclopedia to add more events to your timeline.

Remember to pay attention to location.

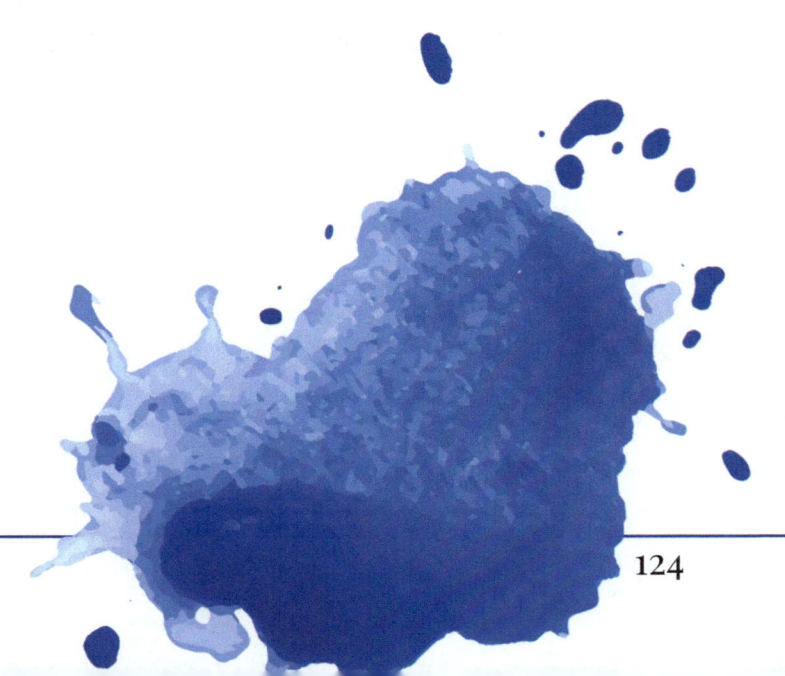

WEEK: 15	**PEOPLE OF CANAAN**		
KEYWORDS:	Canaanites, Sea People, Philistines	**RESOURCES:**	UILE
SKILL:	Summarizing	**PROJECT:**	PowerPoint
MAPPING:	Canaan	**TIMELINING:**	People of Canaan

EXPLANATION

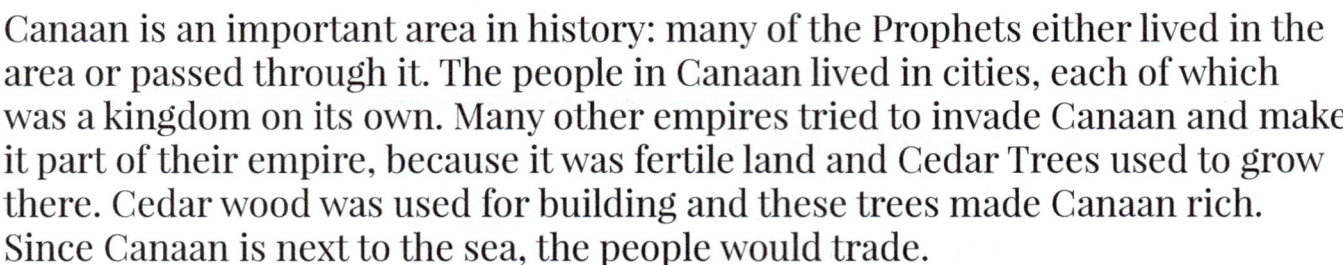

TOPIC: PEOPLE OF CANAAN

Canaan is an important area in history: many of the Prophets either lived in the area or passed through it. The people in Canaan lived in cities, each of which was a kingdom on its own. Many other empires tried to invade Canaan and make it part of their empire, because it was fertile land and Cedar Trees used to grow there. Cedar wood was used for building and these trees made Canaan rich. Since Canaan is next to the sea, the people would trade.

RESEARCH:

Day 1 & 2:

You know what to do!

Find your resources, and read the text. Use the check-list below and the **cheat sheet** to ask yourself the questions.

Check-list:

- Find your resources
- Ask yourself the questions before reading
- Write down difficult words
- Read the text
- Ask yourself the questions during reading
- Ask yourself the questions after reading
- Check in with yourself
- Form your opinion

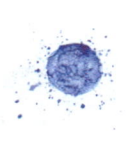

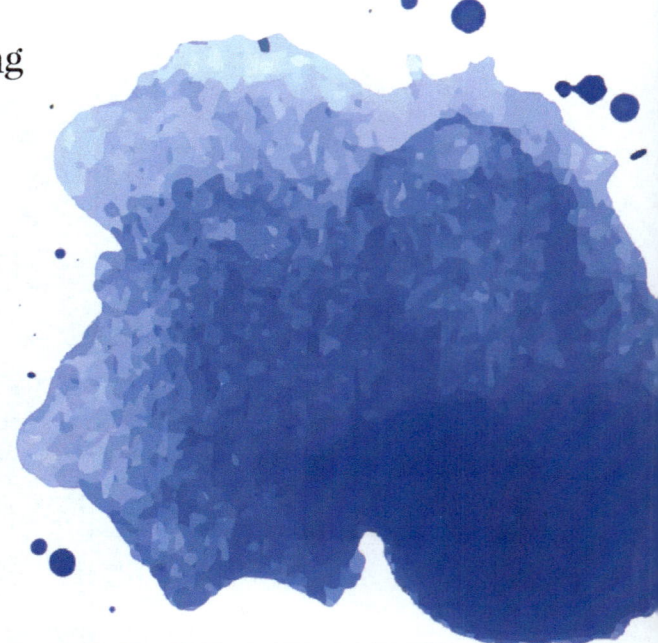

SKILL: SUMMARIZING

A summary is a short version of the text. If you can write a good summary of a text, it means you really did understand it properly. Writing summaries helps with revision of information when you have to study and helps you understand better what you have to study.

By definition, a summary is "a brief statement or account of the main points of something." Writing a good summary indicates that you clearly understand a text and that you can effectively communicate that understanding to your readers. After all, if you really know a subject, you will be able to summarize it. If you cannot summarize a subject, even if you have memorized all the facts about it, you can be absolutely sure that you have not learned it. If you can write a one or two sentence summary after reading a paragraph you have understood the paragraph well.

Steps for making a good summary:

Step1: Read the text without making any notes
Step 2: Think about what you just read
Step 3: Read it again, this time actively
Step 4: Organize the information
Step 5: Write the one or two paragraphs summarizing the text.

Step 1: Read the text without making any notes. Just read it. This allows you to understand the main points of the text better. You will have an overview of all the main points the writer makes.

Step 2: Think about the main points: what is the author trying to tell you? What are you supposed to take away from the text? Think of the What, Where, When, Who, Why and How of the text.

Step 3: Read the text again, this time actively marking important points. Make notes on the main points, underline them in the text if possible. use colors etc. Make sure you mark parts that you find difficult or do not understand well. Reread any parts that were unclear. Remember, often the most important information of a paragraph is in the first or last sentences: the topic sentences.

Step 4: Organize the information you got from actively reading the text. Look at your notes: what stands out? Where are the main points?

SKILL:

Your Turn:

This week, we will focus on step 1 & 2. Read the text (step 1), and think about the main points of the text (step 2).

What is the topic of the text?
What is the author trying to tell you?
How can you tell what the main ideas are?
What is the main event?
Who is the main actor?
When did it happen?
Where did it happen?
Why did it happen?

Write down some of the main ideas in one or two sentences.

Step 5: Write your summary. Remember that it should be shorter than the original text, written in your own words but not show any of your opinions: only show what the author of the text said. Review your summary to make sure it includes all main points, but no unnecessary information.

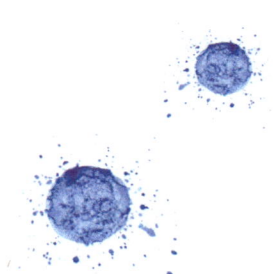

TIPS:
- Write in present tense
- Use your own words
- Do not put your own opinion
- Keep it short

Your Turn:

This week, we will focus on step 1 & 2. Read the text for the day, without making any notes (step 1).

Once you have read it, ask yourself: what is this text trying to tell me?

Write down some of the main ideas in one or two sentences.

Steps for good PPT presentations:

Step 1: Research your topic
Step 2: Make a quick outline
Step 3: Choose a template
Step 4: One main point per slide
Step 5: Keep the design simple

This week, we will focus on all the steps above:

Step 1: Research your topic. The easiest way is to make note of the main points of the topic. Ask yourself the research questions to extract the most important information

Step 2: Write a quick outline on what your PPT is about. Think of who you are writing this presentation for: who is your audience?

Make sure you list the main points. Slides should never contain full paragraphs. Use your own words: do not copy/paste from a text.

Make an introduction. In the introduction you introduce the topic sentence (or thesis) and give a summary of your PPT. Create a conclusion sentence: restate the topic sentence (or thesis) and add a call to action, or a bold statement.

Step 3: Choose a template. There are many template but try to choose one that fits your topic. A slide template can have different lay-outs. Titles can be at the top, left side or right side. There can be space for a graphic (a graph or an image).

Step 4: Use one main point for every slide. Present the information in short sentences or phrases. Use bullet points or numbers to present the information.

Step 5: Design your slide. Keep it simple: clutter will distract from the point you are making.

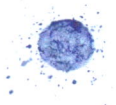

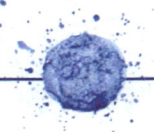

PROJECT:

When picking colors, make sure they are maximum three colors. Use the same colors throughout the presentation. Softer colors are usually good to use, because they do not distract much. However, sometimes bold colors serve the purpose well.

When using graphics, make sure they are of high resolution. Nothing says amateur presentation as much as blurry graphics. Graphics should serve to support the main point of the slide.

Another option in PowerPoint presentations are transitions. Transitions are the movements with which the slides change from one to another. Keep the transitions to a minimum as they may distract from the point of your PPT. If you choose a transition, try to stick with the same one throughout the presentation.

Graphs are wonderful ways to support the point you are trying to make. Ask yourself: what is the one thing, I want the audience to take from this slide? Your graphic should highlight that one thing. Graphs should fit with the design, so pick the same colors.

Your Turn:

You have already researched your topic for this week, so write a quick outline about the main events. Think of a catchy title and a topic sentence.

Pick a template to use for your presentation this week.

Add at least **one image or clip art** to your presentation that supports the main point.

Create a PPT with a minimum of **7 slides:** one introduction slide, 5 main point slides (one main point per slide) and one conclusion slide.

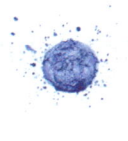

MAP:

Trace the map for the People of Canaan: which map do you need? Where can you find this area on the World Wall Map?

Mark in your map the following:
- Label the seas & oceans
- Mark Byblos
- Shade Canaan
- Mark Egypt

Use the map in the encyclopedia to help you.

Make sure your map is labeled correctly.

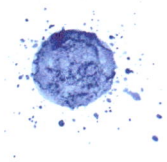

TIMELINE:

Add the People of Canaan to your timeline.

Use the box with dates in the encyclopedia to add more events to your timeline.

Remember to pay attention to location.

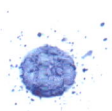

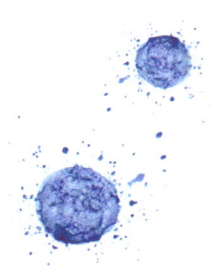

WEEK: 16	PROPHET SHU'AYB (AS), PROPHET MUSA (AS) & THE ISRAELITES		
KEYWORDS:	Prophet Musa (as), Prophet Shu'ayb (as), Israel, Hebrews, Jews	RESOURCES:	UILE HI Super Servants Series
SKILL:	Summarizing	PROJECT:	PowerPoint
MAPPING:	Prophet Musa (as) Prophet Shu'ayb (as)	TIMELINING:	Prophet Musa (as) Prophet Shu'ayb (as)

TOPIC:

Prophet Musa (as) was sent to Bani Israeel. Prophet Musa (as) had to face many challenges dealing with Fir'awn and Bani Israeel. From them came many prophets. However, Bani Israeel were also a disobedient people and eventually angered Allah (swt).

Prophet Shu'ayb (as) was sent to several people. Once the first was destroyed, he was sent to the second place. When the second group was destroyed as well, he settled in Madyan, where he met prophet Musa (as), who became his son-in-law.

RESEARCH:

Day 1 & 2:

You know what to do!

Find your resources, and read the text. Use the check-list below and the **cheat sheet** to ask yourself the questions.

Check-list:

- Find your resources
- Ask yourself the questions before reading
- Write down difficult words
- Read the text
- Ask yourself the questions during reading
- Ask yourself the questions after reading
- Check in with yourself
- Form your opinion

SKILL: SUMMARIZING

Writing a good summary indicates that you clearly understand a text and that you can effectively communicate that understanding to your readers.

Steps for making a good summary:

Step 1: Read the text without making any notes
Step 2: Think about what you just read
Step 3: Read it again, this time actively
Step 4: Organize the information
Step 5: Write the one or two paragraphs summarizing the text.

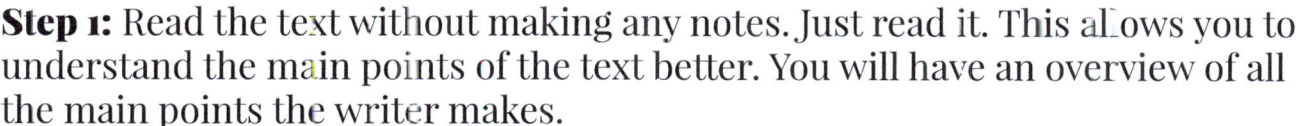

Step 1: Read the text without making any notes. Just read it. This allows you to understand the main points of the text better. You will have an overview of all the main points the writer makes.

Step 2: Think about the main points: what is the author trying to tell you? What re you supposed to take away from the text? Think of the What. Where, When, Who, Why and How of the text.

Step 3: Read the text again, this time actively marking important points. Make notes on the main points, underline them in the text if possible, use colors etc. Make sure you mark parts that you find difficult or do not understand well. Reread any parts that were unclear. Remember, often the most important information of a paragraph is in the first or last sentences: the topic sentences.

Step 4: Organize the information you got from actively reading the text. Look at your notes: what stands out? Where are the main points?

Step 5: Write your summary. Remember that it should be shorter than the original text, written in your own words but not show any of your opinions: only show what the author of the text said. Review your summary to make sure it includes all main points, but no unnecessary information.

TIPS:
*   Write in present tense
*   Use your own words
*   Do not put your own opinion
*   Keep it short

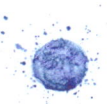

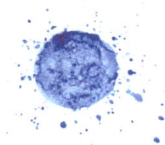

PROJECT: POWERPOINT

Steps for good PPT presentations:

Step 1: Research your topic
Step 2: Make a quick outline
Step 3: Choose a template
Step 4: One main point per slide
Step 5: Keep the design simple

This week, we will focus on all the steps above:

Step 1: Research your topic. The easiest way is to make note of the main points of the topic. Ask yourself the research questions to extract the most important information

Step 2: Write a quick outline on what your PPT is about. Think of who you are writing this presentation for: who is your audience?

Make sure you list the main points.
Make an introduction. Create a conclusion sentence.

Step 3: Choose a template. There are many template but try to choose one that fits your topic. A slide template can have different lay-outs. Titles can be at the top, left side or right side. There can be space for a graphic (a graph or an image).

Step 4: Use one main point for every slide. Present the information in short sentences or phrases. Use bullet points or numbers to present the information.

Step 5: Design your slide. Keep it simple: clutter will distract from the point you are making. Use maximum three colors.

When using graphics, make sure they are of high resolution. Keep the transitions to a minimum as they may distract from the point of your PPT. If you choose a transition, try to stick with the same one throughout the presentation.

PROJECT:

Your Turn:

You have already researched your topic for this week, so write a quick outline about the main events. Think of a catchy title and a topic sentence.

Pick a template to use for your presentation this week.

Add at least one image or clip art to your presentation that supports the main point.

Create a PPT with a minimum of **7 slides:** one introduction slide, 5 main point slides (one main point per slide) and one conclusion slide.

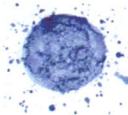

MAP:

Trace the map for the areas where prophet Musa (as) used to live. Which map would you need? Where are these areas located on the World Wall Map?

Mark the following in your map:
- Label the seas and oceans
- Mark Jerusalem
- Mark Madyan
- Mark Sinai
- Mark Egypt

Part 1 of his journey:
- Draw an arrow from Egypt to Madyan, following the coast line in Sinai

Part 2 of his journey:
- Draw an arrow from Madyan back to Egypt, similar to the first one. Use a different color for this arrow.

Part 3 of his journey:
- Draw an arrow from Egypt to Sinai, making it loop in Sinai.
- Draw an arrow from Sinai to Jerusalem

Map of Musa (as)

You can look at the maps on this page for help.

Make sure your map is labeled correctly.

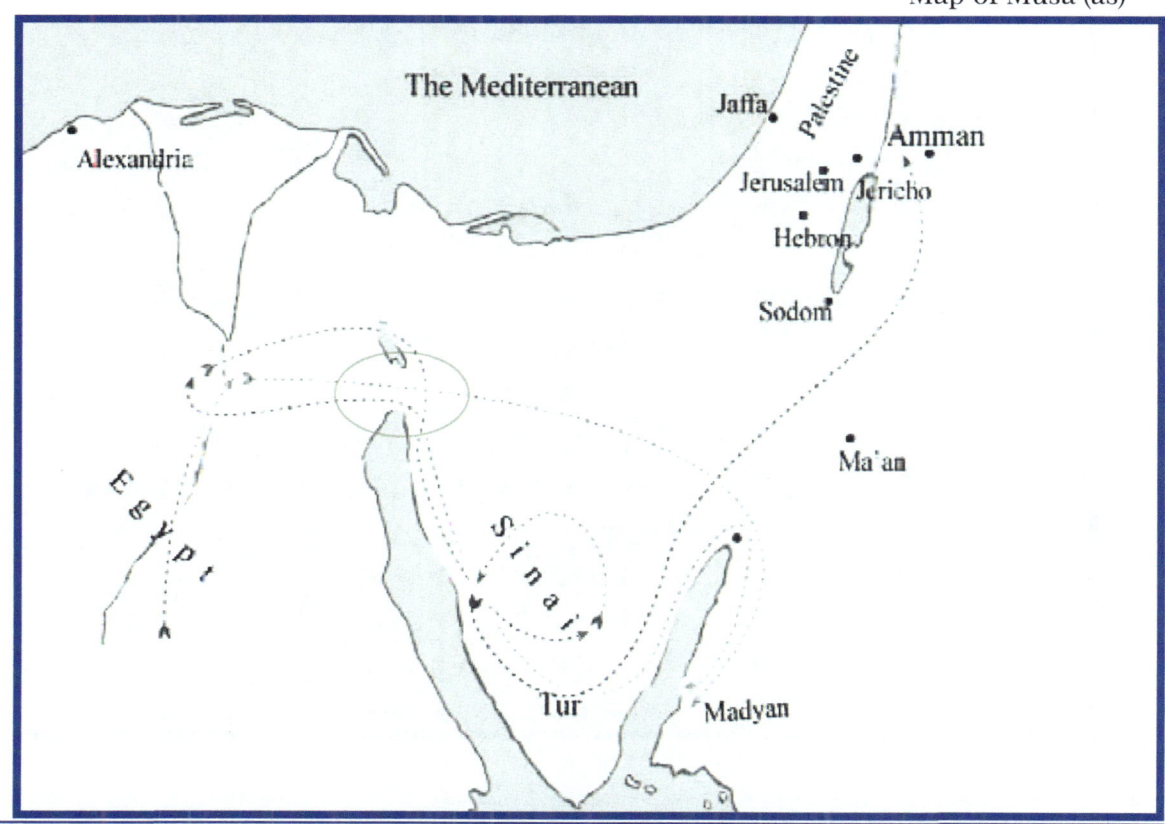

Add Prophet Musa (as) and prophet Shu'ayb (as) to your time line. Pay attention to the location: where would you place him?

See if you can add any significant events from this period to your timeline.

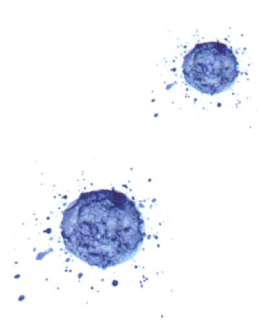

Map of Shu'ayb (as)

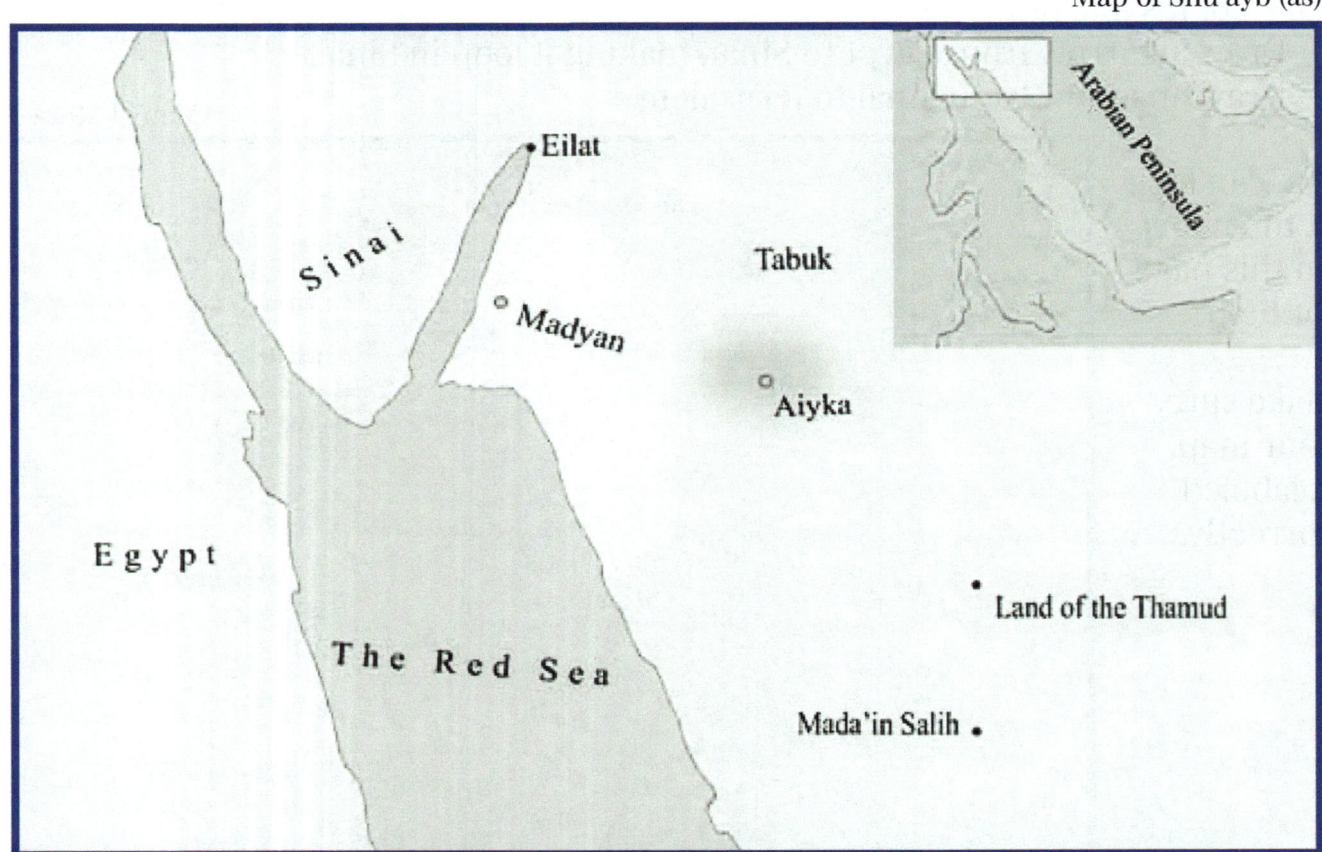

WEEK: 17	**PROPHET DAWUD (AS) & PROPHET SULAYMAN (AS)**		
KEYWORDS:	Prophet Dawud (as), Prophet Sulayman (as)	**RESOURCES:**	HI Super Servants Series
SKILL:	Summarizing	**PROJECT:**	PowerPoint
MAPPING:	Prophet Dawud (as), Prophet Sulayman (as)	**TIMELINING:**	Prophet Dawud (as), Prophet Sulayman (as)

EXPLANATION

TOPIC: PROPHET DAWUD (AS) & PROPHET SULAYMAN (AS)

Both the stories of prophet Dawud (as) and prophet Sulayman (as) are full of important lessons for us to learn. These prophets didn't travel much; they lived in Palestine (Canaan).

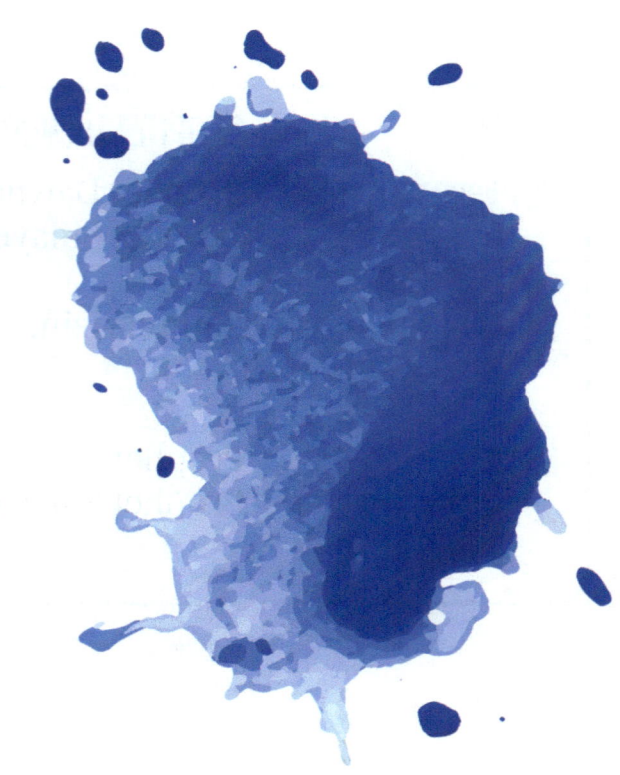

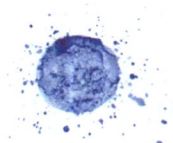

RESEARCH:

Day 1 & 2:

You know what to do!

Find your resources, and read the text. Use the check-list below and the **cheat sheet** to ask yourself the questions.

Check-list:

- Find your resources
- Ask yourself the questions before reading
- Write down difficult words
- Read the text
- Ask yourself the questions during reading
- Ask yourself the questions after reading
- Check in with yourself
- Form your opinion

SKILL: SUMMARIZING

Writing a good summary indicates that you clearly understand a text and that you can effectively communicate that understanding to your readers.

Steps for making a good summary:

Step 1: Read the text without making any notes
Step 2: Think about what you just read
Step 3: Read it again, this time actively
Step 4: Organize the information
Step 5: Write the one or two paragraphs summarizing the text.

Step 1: Read the text without making any notes. Just read it. This allows you to understand the main points of the text better. You will have an overview of all the main points the writer makes.

Step 2: Think about the main points: what is the author trying to tell you? What re you supposed to take away from the text? Think of the What, Where, When, Who, Why and How of the text.

Step 3: Read the text again, this time actively marking important points. Make notes on the main points, underline them in the text if possible, use colors etc. Make sure you mark parts that you find difficult or do not understand well. Reread any parts that were unclear. Remember, often the most important information of a paragraph is in the first or last sentences: the topic sentences.

Step 4: Organize the information you got from actively reading the text. Look at your notes: what stands out? Where are the main points?

Step 5: Write your summary. Remember that it should be shorter than the original text, written in your own words but not show any of your opinions: only show what the author of the text said. Review your summary to make sure it includes all main points, but no unnecessary information.

TIPS:
* Write in present tense
* Use your own words
* Do not put your own opinion
* Keep it short

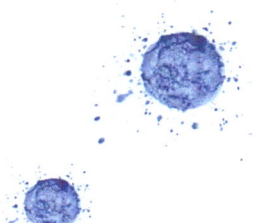

SKILL:

Your Turn:

This week, we will focus on step 1 through 3. Read the text (step 1), and think about the main points of the text (step 2).

Ask yourself the questions (**what, who, when, where, why and how**) and then re-read the text and actively make notes on the main points and difficult parts (Step 3).

Make a summary of the main ideas in one or two sentences.

Steps for good PPT presentations:

Step 1: Research your topic
Step 2: Make a quick outline
Step 3: Choose a template
Step 4: One main point per slide
Step 5: Keep the design simple

This week, we will focus on all the steps above:

Step 1: Research your topic. The easiest way is to make note of the main points of the topic. Ask yourself the research questions to extract the most important information

Step 2: Write a quick outline on what your PPT is about. Think of who you are writing this presentation for: who is your audience?

Make sure you list the main points.
Make an introduction. Create a conclusion sentence.

Step 3: Choose a template. There are many template but try to choose one that fits your topic. A slide template can have different lay-outs. Titles can be at the top, left side or right side. There can be space for a graphic (a graph or an image).

Step 4: Use one main point for every slide. Present the information in short sentences or phrases. Use bullet points or numbers to present the information.

Step 5: Design your slide. Keep it simple: clutter will distract from the point you are making. Use maximum three colors.

When using graphics, make sure they are of high resolution. Keep the transitions to a minimum as they may distract from the point of your PPT. If you choose a transition, try to stick with the same one throughout the presentation.

Your Turn:

You have already researched your topic for this week, so write a quick outline about the main events. Think of a catchy title and a topic sentence.

Pick a template to use for your presentation this week.

Add at least one image or clip art to your presentation that supports the main point.

Create a PPT with a minimum of **7 slides:** one introduction slide, 5 main point slides (one main point per slide) and one conclusion slide. pay attention to the colors you use.

MAP:

Trace the map for the areas where prophets Dawud (as) and Sulayman (as) used to live. Which map would you need? Where is this area located on the World Wall Map?

Mark the following in your map:
- Label the seas and oceans
- Mark Jerusalem
- Shade the kingdom of prophet Dawud (as) and prophet Sulayman (as)

You can look at the map on this page for help.

What do you think the little extra map, in the lower right corner, is showing?

Make sure your map is labeled correctly.

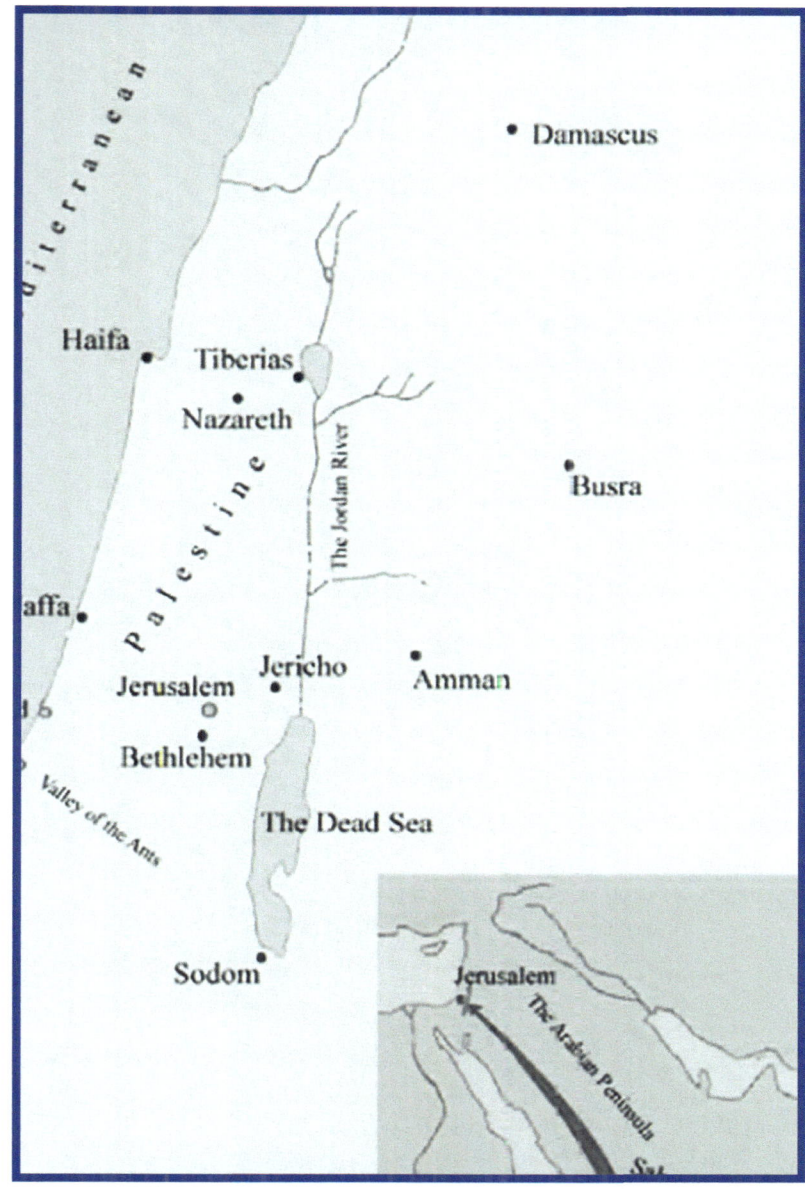

TIMELINE:

Add prophet Dawud (as) and prophet Sulayman (as) to your time line. Pay attention to the location: where would you place them?

Look in the History Intersections, 2nd edition, and see if you can add any other events from this period to your timeline.

WEEK: 18	**PHOENICIANS**		
KEYWORDS:	Phoenicians, Carthage	**RESOURCES:**	UILE
SKILL:	Summarizing	**PROJECT:**	Poster
MAPPING:	Phoenicia	**TIMELINING:**	Phoenicia

EXPLANATION

TOPIC: PHOENICIANS

After many generations, the people of Canaan became the Phoenicians. The Phoenicians had many strong cities with high walls along the coast. They were very good at sailing and built very sturdy ships. With these ships they sailed very far, even all the way around Africa! They built even more cities along the coast of Africa.

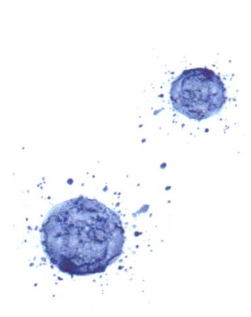

RESEARCH:

Day 1 & 2:

You know what to do!

Find your resources, and read the text. Use the check-list below and the **cheat sheet** to ask yourself the questions.

Check-list:

- Find your resources
- Ask yourself the questions before reading
- Write down difficult words
- Read the text
- Ask yourself the questions during reading
- Ask yourself the questions after reading
- Check in with yourself
- Form your opinion

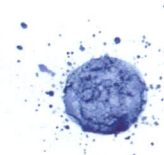

SKILL: SUMMARIZING

Writing a good summary indicates that you clearly understand a text and that you can effectively communicate that understanding to your readers.

Steps for making a good summary:

Step 1: Read the text without making any notes
Step 2: Think about what you just read
Step 3: Read it again, this time actively
Step 4: Organize the information
Step 5: Write the one or two paragraphs summarizing the text.

Step 1: Read the text without making any notes. Just read it. This allows you to understand the main points of the text better. You will have an overview of all the main points the writer makes.

Step 2: Think about the main points: what is the author trying to tell you? What re you supposed to take away from the text? Think of the What, Where, When, Who, Why and How of the text.

Step 3: Read the text again, this time actively marking important points. Make notes on the main points, underline them in the text if possible, use colors etc. Make sure you mark parts that you find difficult or do not understand well. Remember, often the most important information of a paragraph is in the first or last sentences: the topic sentences.

Step 4: Organize the information you got from actively reading the text. Look at your notes: what stands out? Where are the main points?

Step 5: Write your summary. Remember that it should be shorter than the original text, written in your own words but not show any of your opinions: only show what the author of the text said. Review your summary to make sure it includes all main points, but no unnecessary information.

TIPS:
- Write in present tense
- Use your own words
- Do not put your own opinion
- Keep it short

Your Turn:

This week, we will focus on step 1 through 3. Read the text (step 1), and think about the main points of the text (step 2).

Ask yourself the questions (**what, who, when, where, why and how**) and then re-read the text and actively make notes on the main points and difficult parts (Step 3).

Write down some of the main ideas.

PROJECT: POSTER

It has been a while since we did our last poster. Remember the elements?
These are the four elements of a poster:

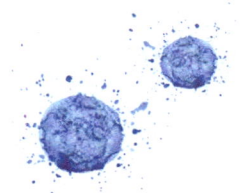

- The Title & Subtitle
- Graphics
- White Space
- Colors

Title:
Your title should tell the reader what your poster is about. Do not use more than two lines for your title. Use 48 point size of the font (the letters) and use them in bold (fat). A subtitle tells you a bit more about the topic, in one short sentence. The subtitle is usually written in a smaller font, directly under the title.

Graphics:
The graphics you choose, have to make sense with the topic. Choose high resolution graphics, over 300 ppi. If you use a table or a figure, always make sure you use a caption (a title for the figure or table).

TIP: Be careful when browsing the web searching for images. Make sure you stick to the mentioned websites, because sometimes when you download an image, there is a computer virus attached to it and it will infect your computer.

Whitespace:
This is one of the **most important** aspects of poster design: the space you leave 'empty'. Whitespace means there is no text. This empty space helps create borders around text, helps organize the information in useful blocks and gives the viewer 'breathing space'.

Colors:
Colors draw attention to a poster and also help organize the information. However, using two colors very similar to each other (called low-contrast colors) together makes it very hard to read the information or see the different parts. Using too many colors will make the poster too overwhelming. Try to stick to no more than three colors and try to make these colors complementary (opposite colors on the color wheel, see in the back for a color wheel).

Every color calls for a specific emotion. Blue is often considered calming, green is fresh, red is vibrant, yellow is happy etc. The colors you use should match your topic. If your poster is telling us about a war, the colors you could use would be black, grey, brown, with some red for example.

Using colors to make certain important things pop is a very clever way of adding color to your poster.

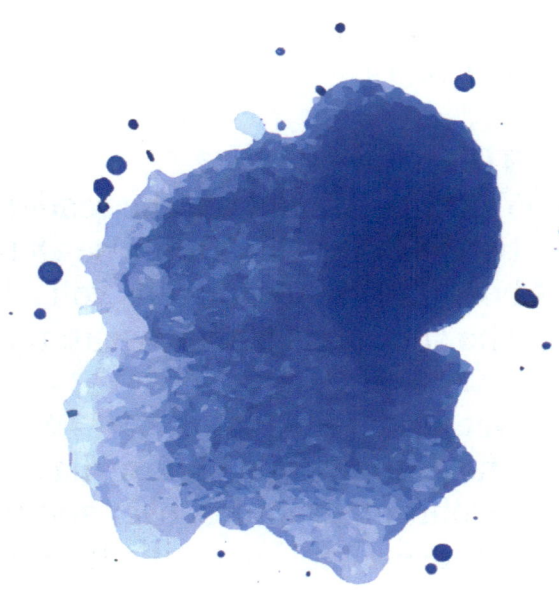

TIP: In order to create a sense that all the parts of the poster fit together, you can use colors similar to the colors in graphics. In order to make something stand out, use a complementary color.

Let's have a look at our poster again.

What are the colors in the poster, other than black and white?

Beige, sand color, brown, and a bit of green.
Canva helps you choose colors that match any images, because they automatically list the colors for each image you use.

What kind of feelings do the colors in this graphic bring?
What pops in this poster?

TIP: when making a poster, make different versions of the same poster: try out different lay-outs, different colors. Save each version and when you have a few, look at them again. Usually, you will like one of the designs more than the others.

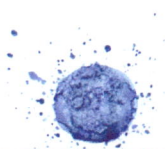

Your Project:

Create your poster for this week. This week, pay special attention to color. Look at the colors in your image/graphic used, and match or complement them. Change the colors in your template. Create three different versions with different colors. Which one works best with the topic of this week?

Requirements: Pick a pre-made template based upon the parts of the poster needed. Add/remove parts as necessary. Title and subtitle should be correct. Image/graphics should match the topic. Whitespace should be used correctly. Colors should be changed: a minimum of three versions with different colors.

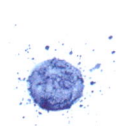

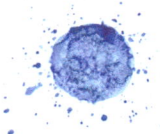

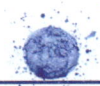

MAP:

Trace the map for the Phoenicians which map do you need? Where can you find this area on the World Wall Map?

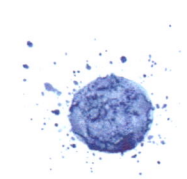

Mark in your map the following:

- Label the seas & oceans
- Mark Tyre
- Mark Carthage
- Draw an arrow from Tyre to Carthage, following the coastline
- Shade Phoenicia
- Shade the areas where Phoenicians settled

Use the map in the encyclopedia to help you.

Make sure your map is labeled correctly.

TIMELINE:

Add the Phoenicians to your timeline.

Use the box with dates in the encyclopedia to add more events to your timeline.

Remember to pay attention to location.

WEEK: 19	ASSYRIANS & PROPHET YUNUS (AS)		
KEYWORDS:	Assyrians, Babylon, Nineveh, Prophet Yunus (as)	RESOURCES:	UILE HI Super Servants Series
SKILL:	Summarizing	PROJECT:	Diagramming
MAPPING:	Prophet Yunus (as)	TIMELINING:	Assyria, Prophet Yunus (as)

EXPLANATION

Day 1:

Eventually, the Assyrians conquered Phoenicia. The Assyrians let Phoenicia basically just live and trade as they had always done.

The Assyrians liked war very much. So much, that they used to go to war every year to conquer new lands. When they would conquer a city, they would make them pay a lot of money and goods to them. If cities did not like that, they were attacked. The Assyrians were very good at attacking cities, even though most cities were protected by high walls. They would have iron weapons instead of bronze ones, and these are much stronger.

Day 2:

Prophet Yunus (as) was born in Nineveh, a city in the Assyrian Empire. Prophet Yunus (as) was submitted to a difficult trial and the dua he made is still used today by Muslims around the world.

RESEARCH:

Day 1 & 2:

You know what to do!

Find your resources, and read the text. Use the check-list below and the **cheat sheet** to ask yourself the questions.

Check-list:

- Find your resources
- Ask yourself the questions before reading
- Write down difficult words
- Read the text
- Ask yourself the questions during reading
- Ask yourself the questions after reading
- Check in with yourself
- Form your opinion

Writing a good summary indicates that you clearly understand a text and that you can effectively communicate that understanding to your readers.

Steps for making a good summary:

Step 1: Read the text without making any notes
Step 2: Think about what you just read
Step 3: Read it again, this time actively
Step 4: Organize the information
Step 5: Write the one or two paragraphs summarizing the text.

Step 1: Read the text without making any notes. Just read it. This allows you to understand the main points of the text better. You will have an overview of all the main points the writer makes.

Step 2: Think about the main points: what is the author trying to tell you? What re you supposed to take away from the text? Think of the What, Where, When, Who, Why and How of the text.

Step 3: Read the text again, this time actively marking important points. Make notes on the main points, underline them in the text if possible, use colors etc. Make sure you mark parts that you find difficult or do not understand well. Remember, often the most important information of a paragraph is in the first or last sentences: the topic sentences.

Step 4: Organize the information you got from actively reading the text. Look at your notes: what stands out? Where are the main points?

Step 5: Write your summary. Remember that it should be shorter than the original text, written in your own words but not show any of your opinions: only show what the author of the text said. Review your summary to make sure it includes all main points, but no unnecessary information.

TIPS:
- Write in present tense
- Use your own words
- Do not put your own opinion
- Keep it short

SKILL:

Your Turn:

This week, we will focus on all steps. Read the text (step 1), and think about the main points of the text (step 2).

Ask yourself the questions (**what, who, when, where, why and how**) and then re-read the text and actively make notes on the main points and difficult parts.

Read the text again (step 3), this time jotting down notes. Look at your notes: what are the main points? (step 4)

Make a summary of the main ideas in **one paragraph** (step 5).

PROJECT: DIAGRAMMING

Remember how making diagram means you show information in a visual form? We will do another diagram this week.

5 Easy Steps to make a diagram:

Step 1: Look at what information you have: how does it relate to each other?
Step 2: Look at the diagrams: what relationship does each diagram show?
Step 3: Choose a diagram that fits your information
Step 4: Draw the diagram
Step 5: Add the information in the diagram

All parts of the diagram need to be labeled. Your drawing does not need to be perfect, but needs to show the problem and your thought process.

Your Turn:

Diagram the events of the journey Prophet Yunus (as).
Use the the image on the this page to choose a diagram and use 5 steps above to guide you in making your diagram.

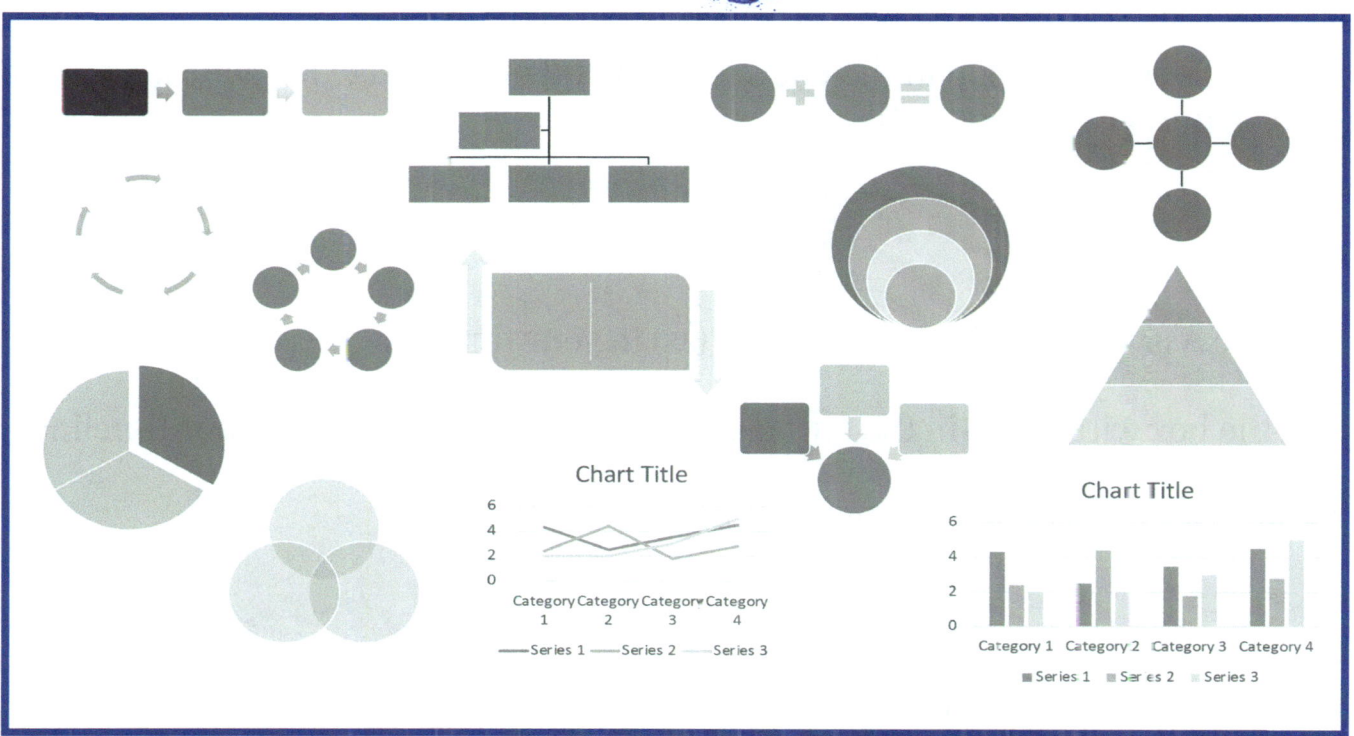

MAP:

Trace the map for Prophet Yunus (as): which map do you need? Where can you find this area on the World Wall Map?

Mark in your map the following:
- Label the seas & oceans
- Mark Babylon
- Mark Nineveh
- Shade the area of the Assyrian Empire
- Mark Aleppo
- Mark Jaffa (close to Jerusalem)
- Draw an arrow from Nineveh to Aleppo
- Draw an arrow from Aleppo to Jaffa

You can look at the map in the encyclopedia and on this page for help. Make sure your map is labeled correctly.

TIMELINE:

Add the Assyrians and Prophet Yunus (as) to your timeline.

Use the box with dates in the encyclopedia to add more events to your timeline.

Remember to pay attention to location.

WEEK: 20	BABYLONIANS		
KEYWORDS:	Babylon, Nebuchadnezzar Prophet Uzair (as)	RESOURCES:	UILE HI
SKILL:	Summarizing	PROJECT:	Poster
MAPPING:	Babylon	TIMELINING:	Babylon

EXPLANATION

TOPIC: BABYLONIANS

Remember the empire of Hammurabi; the one who wrote down the laws on a tablet? His empire was called Babylon. After a while, the Assyrians conquered the empire of Hammurabi. As we have seen the Assyrians love war.

Then one day, a general of the Babylonian army made himself king and fought off the Assyrians. With his son Nebuchadnezzar II, he built the city of Babylon. Nebuchadnezzar fought many wars and built a large empire. Eventually the Persians came and destroyed Babylon and it became part of Persia.

Nebuchadnezzar often raided Jerusalem and took the Jews as slaves. Read the story of prophet Uzair (as) this week as well.

RESEARCH:

Day 1 & 2:

You know what to do!

Find your resources, and read the text. Use the check-list below and the **cheat sheet** to ask yourself the questions.

Check-list:

- Find your resources
- Ask yourself the questions before reading
- Write down difficult words
- Read the text
- Ask yourself the questions during reading
- Ask yourself the questions after reading
- Check in with yourself
- Form your opinion

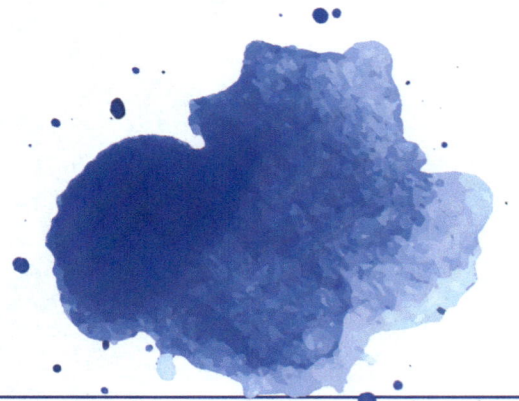

Writing a good summary indicates that you clearly understand a text and that you can effectively communicate that understanding to your readers.

Steps for making a good summary:

Step 1: Read the text without making any notes
Step 2: Think about what you just read
Step 3: Read it again, this time actively
Step 4: Organize the information
Step 5: Write the one or two paragraphs summarizing the text.

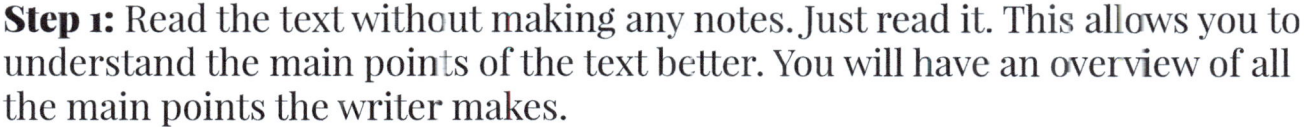

Step 1: Read the text without making any notes. Just read it. This allows you to understand the main points of the text better. You will have an overview of all the main points the writer makes.

Step 2: Think about the main points: what is the author trying to tell you? What re you supposed to take away from the text? Think of the What, Where, When, Who, Why and How of the text.

Step 3: Read the text again, this time actively marking important points. Make notes on the main points, underline them in the text if possible, use colors etc. Make sure you mark parts that you find difficult or do not understand well. Remember, often the most important information of a paragraph is in the first or last sentences: the topic sentences.

Step 4: Organize the information you got from actively reading the text. Look at your notes: what stands out? Where are the main points?

Step 5: Write your summary. Remember that it should be shorter than the original text, written in your own words but not show any of your opinions: only show what the author of the text said. Review your summary to make sure it includes all main points, but no unnecessary information.

TIPS:
*   Write in present tense
*   Use your own words
*   Do not put your own opinion
*   Keep it short

Your Turn:

This week, we will focus on all steps. Read the text (step 1), and think about the main points of the text (step 2).

Ask yourself the questions (**what, who, when, where, why and how**) and then re-read the text and actively make notes on the main points and difficult parts.

Read the text again (step 3), this time jotting down notes. Look at your notes: what are the main points? (step 4)

Make a summary of the main ideas in **one paragraph** (step 5).

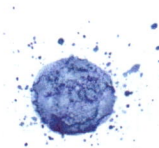

PROJECT: POSTER

Let's do another poster!
These are the four elements of a poster:

- The Title & Subtitle
- Graphics
- White Space
- Colors

Title:
Your title should tell the reader what your poster is about. Do not use more than two lines for your title. Use 48 point size of the font (the letters) and use them in bold (fat). A subtitle tells you a bit more about the topic, in one short sentence. The subtitle is usually written in a smaller font, directly under the title.

Graphics:
The graphics you choose, have to make sense with the topic. Choose high resolution graphics, over 300 ppi. If you use a table or a figure, always make sure you use a caption (a title for the figure or table).

TIP: Be careful when browsing the web searching for images. Make sure you stick to the mentioned websites, because sometimes when you download an

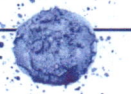

PROJECT:

image, there is a computer virus attached to it and it will infect your computer.

Whitespace:

This is one of the **most important** aspects of poster design: the space you leave 'empty'. Whitespace means there is no text. This empty space helps create borders around text, helps organize the information is useful blocks and gives the viewer 'breathing space'.

Colors:

Colors draw attention to a poster and also help organize the information. However, using two colors very similar to each other (called low-contrast colors) together makes it very hard to read the information or see the different parts. Using too many colors will make the poster too overwhelming. Try to stick to no more than three colors and try to make these colors complementary (opposite colors on the color wheel, see in the back for a color wheel).

Every color calls for a specific emotion. Blue is often considered calming, green is fresh, red is vibrant, yellow is happy etc. The colors you use should match your topic. If your poster is telling us about a war, the colors you could use would be black, grey, brown, with some red for example.

Using colors to make certain important things pop is a very clever way of adding color to your poster.

TIP: In order to create a sense that all the parts of the poster fit together, you can use colors similar to the colors in graphics. In order to make something stand out, use a complementary color.

Let's have a look at our poster again.

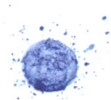

What are the colors in this poster, other than black and white?

Beige, sand color, brown, and a bit of green. Canva helps you choose colors that match any images, because they automatically list the colors for each image you use.

What kind of feelings do the colors in this graphic bring?
What pops in this poster?

TIP: when making a poster, make different versions of the same poster: try out different lay-outs, different colors. Save each version and when you have a few, look at them again. Usually, you will like one of the designs more than the others.

Your Project:

Create your poster for this week. This week, pay special attention to color. Look at the colors in your image/graphic used, and match or complement them. Change the colors in your template. Create three different versions with different colors. Which one works best with the topic of this week?

Requirements: Pick a pre-made template based upon the parts of the poster needed. Add/remove parts as necessary. Title and subtitle should be correct. Image/graphics should match the topic. Whitespace should be used correctly. Colors should be changed: a minimum of three versions with different colors.

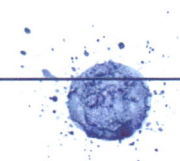

MAP:

Trace the map for the Babylonians: which map do you need? Where can you find this area on the World Wall Map?

Mark in your map the following:
- Label the seas & oceans
- Mark Babylon
- Shade the area of the Babylonian Empire
- Mark Media
- Mark Judah

Use the map in the encyclopedia to help you.

Make sure your map is labeled correctly.

TIMELINE:

Add the Babylonians to your timeline.

Use the box with dates in the encyclopedia to add more events to your timeline.

Remember to pay attention to location.

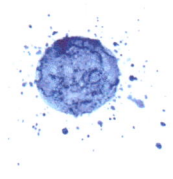
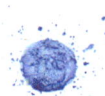

WEEK: 21	PERSIANS & GREEKS		
KEYWORDS:	Persia, Persepolis. King Darius, Media, Athens, Sparta	RESOURCES:	UILE
SKILL:	Summarizing	PROJECT:	Diagramming
MAPPING:	Persia, Greece	TIMELINING:	Persia, Greece

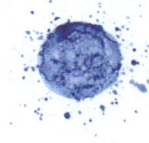

EXPLANATION

TOPIC:

Day 1:

Babylon was conquered by Persia. Persia was a huge empire, larger than any empire ever before. The king of this empire was Darius I. Darius was now faced with ruling a very large empire, with people that were conquered by war and did not really like the Persians much. But Darius was very smart: he would leave the leaders of these people still in charge, and they would have to pay Darius taxes. So Darius became fabulously rich!

Day 2:

As always, one empire grows by destroying another one. After the Myceneans, the Greeks had a very hard life. They spent such a long time trying to survive, that they forgot what they used to do, such as writing and education. This is called the Greek Dark Ages. After a while, they started to trade with other places and they became more wealthy again. They lived in city-states: every city had their own ruler, like a mini kingdom. The two most important city-states were Sparta and Athens. They fought with the Persians and eventually destroyed them.

RESEARCH:

Day 1 & 2:

You know what to do!

Find your resources, and read the text. Use the check-list below and the **cheat sheet** to ask yourself the questions.

Check-list:

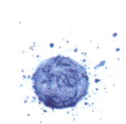

- Find your resources
- Ask yourself the questions before reading
- Write down difficult words
- Read the text
- Ask yourself the questions during reading
- Ask yourself the questions after reading
- Check in with yourself
- Form your opinion

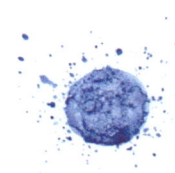

SKILL: SUMMARIZING

Writing a good summary indicates that you clearly understand a text and that you can effectively communicate that understanding to your readers.

Steps for making a good summary:

Step 1: Read the text without making any notes
Step 2: Think about what you just read
Step 3: Read it again, this time actively
Step 4: Organize the information
Step 5: Write the one or two paragraphs summarizing the text.

Step 1: Read the text without making any notes. Just read it. This allows you to understand the main points of the text better. You will have an overview of all the main points the writer makes.

Step 2: Think about the main points: what is the author trying to tell you? What re you supposed to take away from the text? Think of the What, Where, When, Who, Why and How of the text.

Step 3: Read the text again, this time actively marking important points. Make notes on the main points, underline them in the text if possible, use colors etc. Make sure you mark parts that you find difficult or do not understand well. Remember, often the most important information of a paragraph is in the first or last sentences: the topic sentences.

Step 4: Organize the information you got from actively reading the text. Look at your notes: what stands out? Where are the main points?

Step 5: Write your summary. Remember that it should be shorter than the original text, written in your own words but not show any of your opinions: only show what the author of the text said. Review your summary to make sure it includes all main points, but no unnecessary information.

TIPS:
- Write in present tense
- Use your own words
- Do not put your own opinion
- Keep it short

Your Turn:

This week, we will focus on all steps. Read the text (step 1), and think about the main points of the text (step 2).

Ask yourself the questions (**what, who, when, where, why and how**) and then re-read the text and actively make notes on the main points and difficult parts.

Read the text again (step 3), this time jotting down notes. Look at your notes: what are the main points? (step 4)

Make a summary of the main ideas in **one paragraph** (step 5).

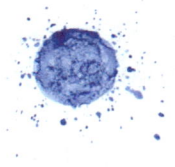

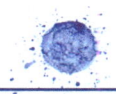

PROJECT: DIAGRAMMING

Remember how making diagram means you show information in a visual form? We will do another diagram this week.

5 Easy Steps to make a diagram:

Step 1: Look at what information you have: how does it relate to each other?
Step 2: Look at the diagrams: what relationship does each diagram show?
Step 3: Choose a diagram that fits your information
Step 4: Draw the diagram
Step 5: Add the information in the diagram

All parts of the diagram need to be labeled. Your drawing does not need to be perfect, but needs to show the problem and your thought process.

Your Turn:

Diagram the culture of Persia. The Persian culture was very unique in many ways: from the inventions like the Royal Road, Palace of Persepolis and more.

Use the image on the this page to choose a diagram and use 5 steps above to guide you in making your diagram.

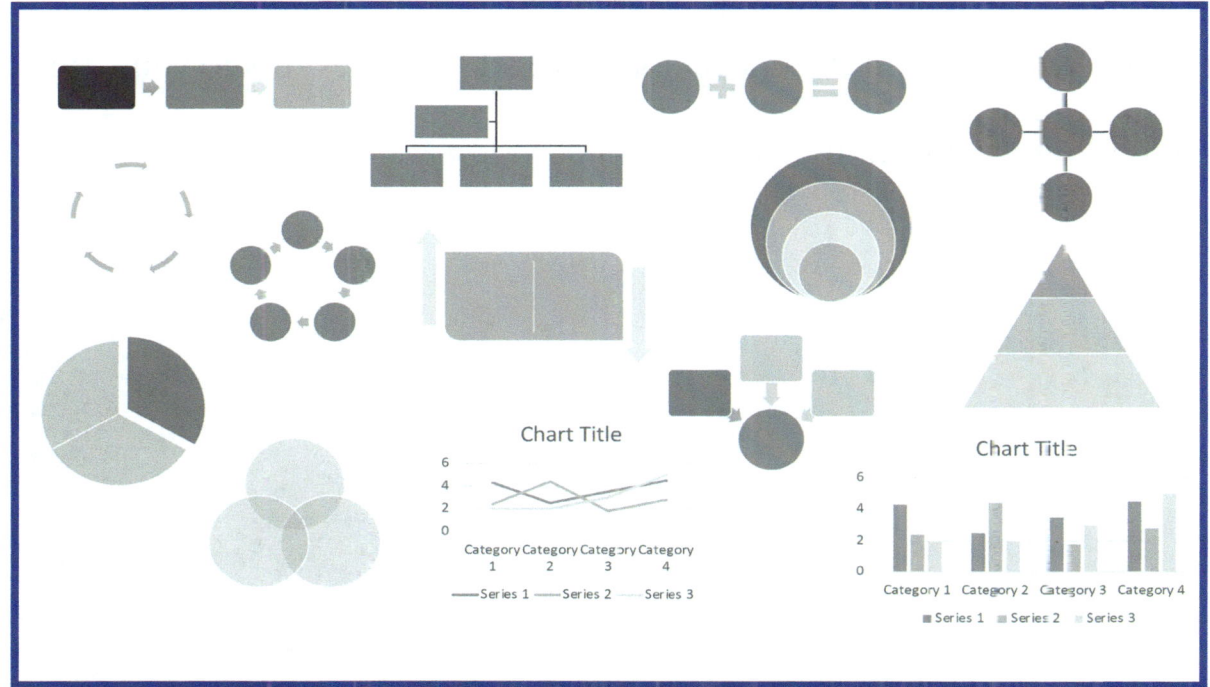

MAP:

Trace the map for the Persians & the Greeks: which map do you need to add them both? Where can you find this area on the World Wall Map?

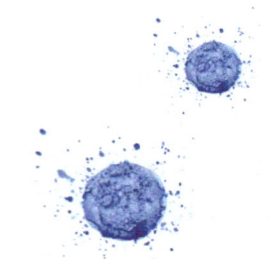

Mark in your map the following:
- Label the seas & oceans
- Mark Babylon
- Mark Persepolis
- Find the Indus River
- Find Egypt
- Shade the area of the Persian Empire
- Mark Athens
- Mark Sparta

Use the map in the encyclopedia to help you.

Make sure your map is labeled correctly.

TIMELINE:

Add the Persians to your timeline.

Use the box with dates in the encyclopedia to add more events to your timeline.

Remember to pay attention to location.

WEEK: 22	**GREECE**		
KEYWORDS:	Greece, Athens, Sparta, Alexander the Great	**RESOURCES:**	UILE
SKILL:	Mind Map	**PROJECT:**	Diagramming
MAPPING:	Greece	**TIMELINING:**	Greece

EXPLANATION

TOPIC: GREECE

Day 1:

We know that the cities in Greece were little kingdoms by themselves. Sparta was a large city where the men were raised as very tough warriors. Athens on the other hand, was focused on knowledge and education. Athens was afraid that the Persians would attack again and convinced other cities to join them to become a larger and stronger group to fight off the Persians.

Day 2:

In the end, Athens was defeated, but all of the cities in Greece were now poor and tired. Even after the Peloponnesian War, the cities in Greece kept fighting a bit with each other. They were so busy fighting each other, that they did not notice that another kingdom was growing stronger: Macedonia. The King of Macedonia, King Philip II, was training his soldiers and building a big army. Eventually, they took all of the Greek city-states and made it into one big kingdom. The son of King Philip II, Alexander, would become one of the world's most famous conquerors.

RESEARCH:

You know what to do!

Find your resources, and read the text. Use the check-list below and the **cheat sheet** to ask yourself the questions.

Check-list:

- Find your resources
- Ask yourself the questions before reading
- Write down difficult words
- Read the text
- Ask yourself the questions during reading
- Ask yourself the questions after reading
- Check in with yourself
- Form your opinion

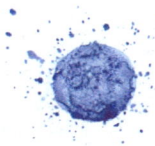

SKILL: MIND MAP

Mind mapping means you make a map of thoughts or pieces of information. Mind maps help you understand, organize and memorize information. They help you get an overview on more complex ideas and they can stimulate your creativity. Mind maps help students save time studying and help prepare for exams. Because the mind map forces you to think radially, you often uncover wider and more interesting ideas.

There are many situations in which you could use a mind map:
- Brainstorming,
- Organizing ideas or concepts
- Solving problems
- Memorizing notes
- Planning
- Managing time
- Goal setting

And many more...

Before you mind map:

Since we use mind maps to organize and understand information from a text, we start by looking at that information. Get a stack of sticky notes. As you read the text, write down the important ideas in one word on the sticky notes: one idea per sticky note. Now briefly summarize the idea under the word.

Stick your sticky notes on the wall (or a door, window, desk etc). Group similar main points together, this is called clustering. See if you can name the category of each cluster of sticky notes. If one cluster becomes very large, think how you can split it into two or more smaller clusters.

If you are not sure how to group the sticky notes into clusters, try asking yourself the What? Where? When? Why? Who? and How? Questions.

As you read the text and think about where new topics may fit in, you will find that the topic starts to take more form in your mind.

TIP: Use a 'parking space' where you place sticky notes that you do not know where to place temporarily. Make sure by the end, all sticky notes are in clusters.

179

Once you are done with the sticky notes, you are ready to put these clusters in a mind map.

Steps of Mind Mapping:

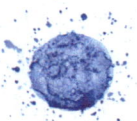

Step 1: Write a **central idea** in a circle or draw an image on the middle of a blank sheet.

TIP: we recommend you use a pencil for the first draft of the mind map, so you can change things as you go along. Later on, you will fill in the branches and sub-branches with colors and images.

Step 2: Draw **thick branches** out from the center word or image. The number of branches depends on the number of clusters you created with the sticky notes. Each cluster will be one branch.

Step 3: Write one keyword on each branch: the word for the category of that cluster.

TIP: you can use CAPS for the main branches and lower-case letters for the sub-branches

Step 4: From every one of these main branches, draw **thinner branches**, like in a tree. Each of these thinner branches is a sub-topic. Write a key word on each of these thinner branches. You can continue splitting up branches into smaller branches as much as you need to show the information.

However, usually mind maps do not go beyond the third level as it will become very cluttered. Remember, the topics of the sub-branches should be included in the topic of the main branches.

Step 5: Use a different color for each main branch (and its sub-branches) to help you organize the clusters. Use images or symbols to help your remember the topics more vividly.

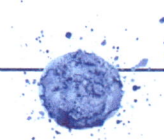

TIP: Use a parking list on the side, for topics that are unclear where they fit in the mind map. You can always add these later. Sometimes, having several ideas in a parking list means you may have to research the topic a bit more.

Your Turn:

As you read, use sticky notes to make clusters of important points. Think of a name for each cluster.

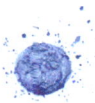

- Sketch the central idea and the main branches.
- Use key words on each branch
- Use colors.

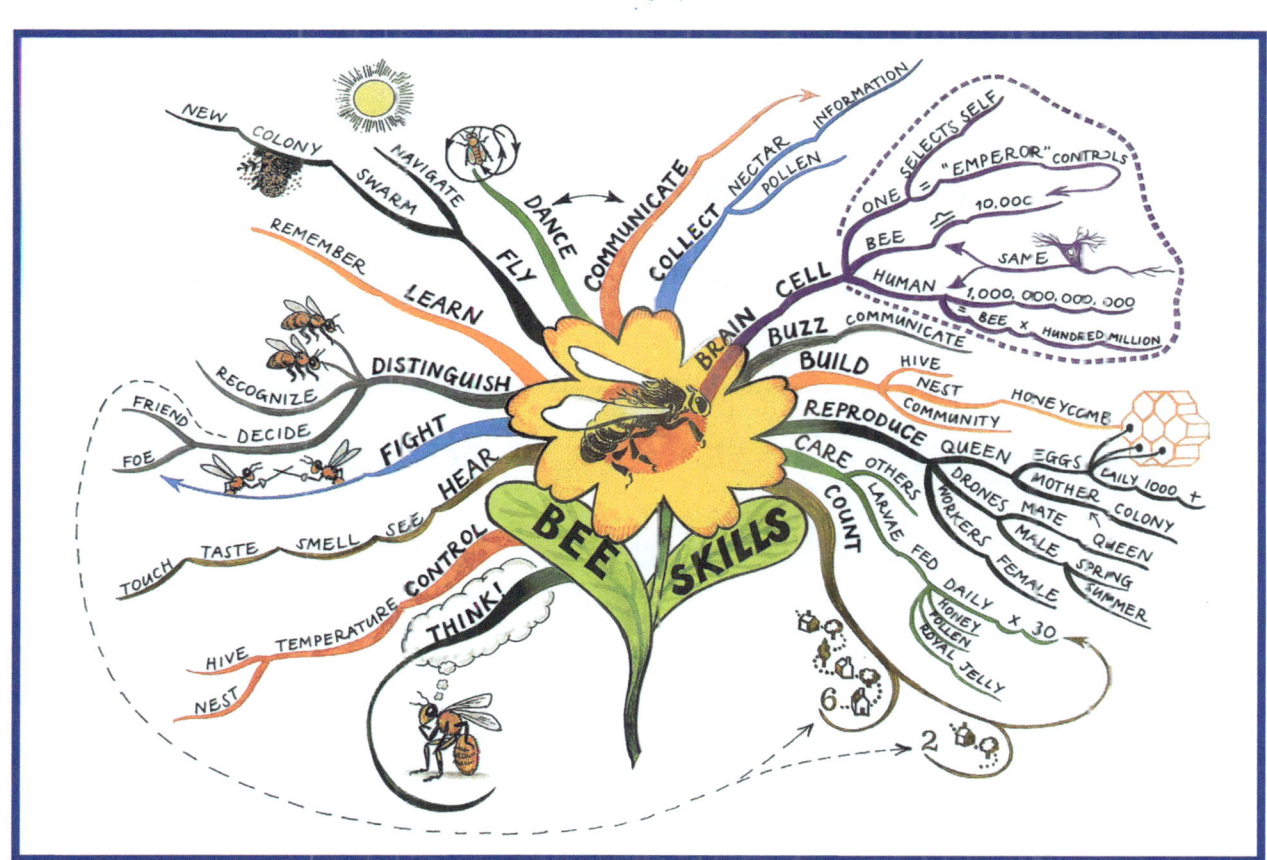

From The Ultimate Book of Mind Mapping by Tony Buzan

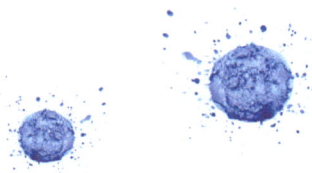

PROJECT: DIAGRAMMING

We will do another diagram this week.

5 Easy Steps to make a diagram:

Step 1: Look at what information you have: how does it relate to each other?
Step 2: Look at the diagrams: what relationship does each diagram show?
Step 3: Choose a diagram that fits your information
Step 4: Draw the diagram
Step 5: Add the information in the diagram

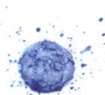

All parts of the diagram need to be labeled. Your drawing does not need to be perfect, but needs to show the problem and your thought process.

Your Turn:

This week, make a Venn Diagram (see the circled diagram below) to show the differences and similarities between Athens and Sparta. Each circle is one item, in this case each city gets its own circle. In the circles you write the differences between the cities. Where they overlap, you write the similarities.

Use the 5 steps above to guide you in making your diagram.

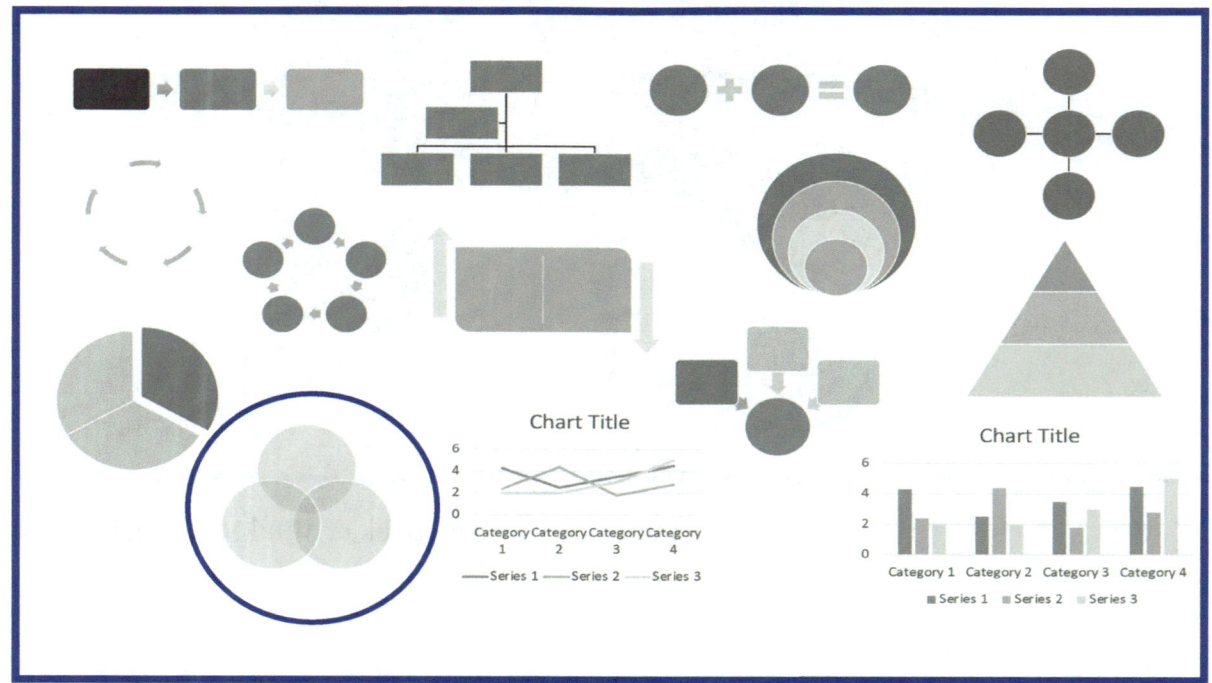

MAP:

Trace the map for the conquests of Alexander the Great: which map do you need? Where can you find this area on the World Wall Map?

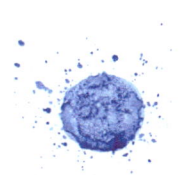

Mark in your map the following:
- Label the seas & oceans
- Mark Macedonia
- Mark Persia
- Mark Egypt
- Mark India
- Shade the area of Alexander's Empire.

Use the map in the encyclopedia to help you.

Make sure your map is labeled correctly.

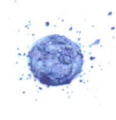 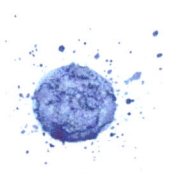

TIMELINE:

Add Alexander the Great to your timeline.

Use the box with dates in the encyclopedia to add more events to your timeline.

Remember to pay attention to location.

WEEK: 23	**CHINA**		
KEYWORDS:	Yellow River, Shang Dynasty, Zhou, Qin Dynasty, Han Dynasty	**RESOURCES:**	UILE
SKILL:	Mind Map	**PROJECT:**	Mind Map
MAPPING:	Ancient China	**TIMELINING:**	Ancient China

EXPLANATION

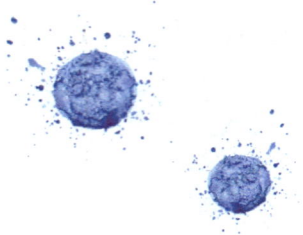

TOPIC:

Just like in Mesopotamia, people in China started to live near the rivers from early on. Next to the rivers they would have water and they could grow food. The biggest river in China is the Yellow River. China was ruled by families, also called dynasties. At first the family of Shang ruled, then Zhou, then Qin (chin) and then Han. Every family could rule for hundreds of years: the son inheriting the throne from his father.

RESEARCH:

You know what to do!

Find your resources, and read the text. Use the check-list below and the **cheat sheet** to ask yourself the questions.

Check-list:

- Find your resources
- Ask yourself the questions before reading
- Write down difficult words
- Read the text
- Ask yourself the questions during reading
- Ask yourself the questions after reading
- Check in with yourself
- Form your opinion

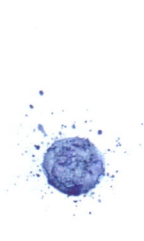

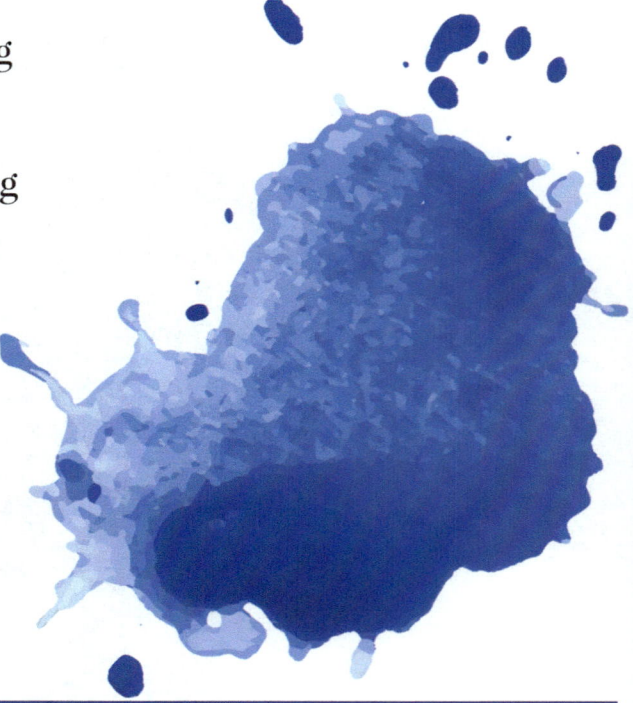

NEW!

Mind mapping means you make a map of thoughts or pieces of information. Mind maps help you understand, organize and memorize information. They help you get an overview on more complex ideas and they can stimulate your creativity. Mind maps help students save time studying and help prepare for exams. Because the mind map forces you to think radially, you often uncover wider and more interesting ideas.

There are many situations in which you could use a mind map:
- Brainstorming,
- Organizing ideas or concepts
- Solving problems
- Memorizing notes
- Planning
- Managing time
- Goal setting

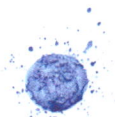
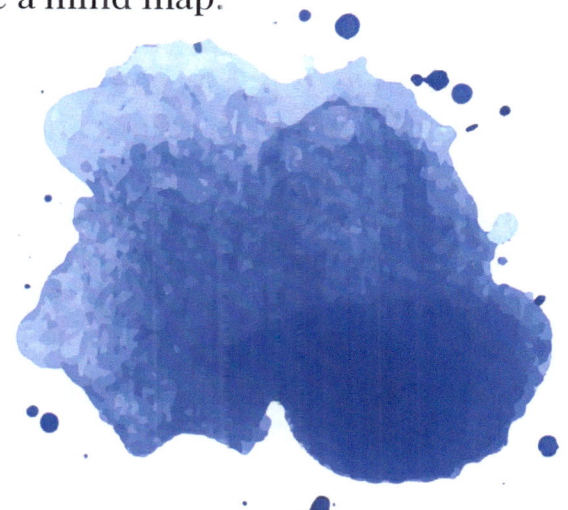

And many more...

Before you mind map:

Since we use mind maps to organize and understand information from a text, we start by looking at that information. Get a stack of sticky notes. As you read the text, write down the important ideas in one word on the sticky notes: one idea per sticky note. Now briefly summarize the idea under the word.

Stick your sticky notes on the wall (or a door, window, desk etc). Group similar main points together, this is called clustering. See if you can name the category of each cluster of sticky notes. If one cluster becomes very large, think how you can split it into two or more smaller clusters.

If you are not sure how to group the sticky notes into clusters, try asking yourself the What? Where? When? Why? Who? and How? Questions.

As you read the text and think about where new topics may fit in, you will find that the topic starts to take more form in your mind.

TIP: Use a 'parking space' where you place sticky notes that you do not know where to place temporarily. Make sure by the end, all sticky notes are in clusters.

Once you are done with the sticky notes, you are ready to put these clusters in a mind map.

Steps of Mind Mapping:

Step 1: Write a **central idea** in a circle or draw an image on the middle of a blank sheet.

TIP: we recommend you use a pencil for the first draft of the mind map, so you can change things as you go along. Later on, you will fill in the branches and sub-branches with colors and images.

Step 2: Draw **thick branches** out from the center word or image. The number of branches depends on the number of clusters you created with the sticky notes. Each cluster will be one branch.

Step 3: Write one keyword on each branch: the word for the category of that cluster.

TIP: you can use CAPS for the main branches and lower-case letters for the sub-branches

Step 4: From every one of these main branches, draw **thinner branches**, like in a tree. Each of these thinner branches is a sub-topic. Write a key word on each of these thinner branches. You can continue splitting up branches into smaller branches as much as you need to show the information.

However, usually mind maps do not go beyond the third level as it will become very cluttered. Remember, the topics of the sub-branches should be included in the topic of the main branches.

Step 5: Use a different color for each main branch (and its sub-branches) to help you organize the clusters. Use images or symbols to help your remember the topics more vividly.

TIP: Use a parking list on the side, for topics that are unclear where they fit in the mind map. You can always add these later. Sometimes, having several ideas in a parking list means you may have to research the topic a bit more.

Clouds:

Sometimes, ideas are truly related to the main topic, but do not find a place on the branches. It is possible to put them in their own bubble or cloud in the margins of the mind map, without any connections to the branches. However, having many clouds in your map, might mean that you have to research your topic a bit more.

Works of Art

Some mind maps are truly works of art, with many drawings and images embedded in the map. Once you have sketched out your basic mind map, take your time to add colors and images.

When you mind map, we want you to take your time. First you organize your information with sticky notes. Then, you will sketch your mind map. Lastly, make your mind map look pretty: use colors and images.

Up until now, you have spent time on practicing a skill and working on a project separately. Now, you will use both these time slots to work on one mind map, so make it something amazing!

Did you know: Mind Mapping is a really cool skill you can use to understand, organize or plan anything? Check out the map below on planning family events.

Your Turn:

As you read, use sticky notes to make clusters of important points. Think of a name for each cluster.

- Sketch the central idea and the main branches.
- **Add on a level of sub-branches with sub-topics.**
- Use key words on each branch
- Use colors.

From The Ultimate Book of Mind Mapping by Tony Buzan

MAP:

Trace the map for Ancient China: which map do you need? Where can you find this area on the World Wall Map?

Mark in your map the following:
- Label the seas & oceans
- Trace the Yellow River
- Trace the Yangtze River
- Mark the Great Wall
- Shade the area of The Qin Dynasty

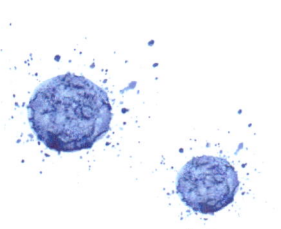

Use the map in the encyclopedia to help you.

Make sure your map is labeled correctly.

TIMELINE:

Add Ancient China to your timeline.

Use the box with dates in the encyclopedia to add more events to your timeline.

Remember to pay attention to location.

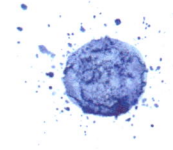

WEEK: 24	**AFRICA**		
KEYWORDS:	People of Nok, Kingdom of Kush, Kingdom of Axum	**RESOURCES:**	UILE
SKILL:	Mind Map	**PROJECT:**	Mind Map
MAPPING:	Africa	**TIMELINING:**	Africa

EXPLANATION

TOPIC: AFRICA

Africa is not a country. It is a large continent with many different countries, like Europe or Asia. In the top of Africa, there is now a large stretch of sand: hot dry sand. This is called the Sahara Desert. Nothing really grows there. The Sahara desert cuts the continent of Africa into two: the top part above the desert is called North Africa and the bottom part, below the desert, is call Sub-Sahara Africa. It was very hard to cross this vast landscape of only sand and sun, so the people at the top developed very differently than the people at the bottom.

RESEARCH:

You know what to do!

Find your resources, and read the text. Use the check-list below and the **cheat sheet** to ask yourself the questions.

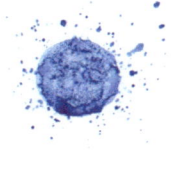

Check-list:

- Find your resources
- Ask yourself the questions before reading
- Write down difficult words
- Read the text
- Ask yourself the questions during reading
- Ask yourself the questions after reading
- Check in with yourself
- Form your opinion

SKILL & PROJECT:

Mind mapping means you make a map of thoughts or pieces of information. Mind maps help you understand, organize and memorize information. They help you get an overview on more complex ideas and they can stimulate your creativity. Mind maps help students save time studying and help prepare for exams. Because the mind map forces you to think radially, you often uncover wider and more interesting ideas.

There are many situations in which you could use a mind map:
- Brainstorming,
- Organizing ideas or concepts
- Solving problems
- Memorizing notes
- Planning
- Managing time
- Goal setting

And many more...

Before you mind map:

Since we use mind maps to organize and understand information from a text, we start by looking at that information. Get a stack of sticky notes. As you read the text, write down the important ideas in one word on the sticky notes: one idea per sticky note. Now briefly summarize the idea under the word.

Stick your sticky notes on the wall (or a door, window, desk etc). Group similar main points together, this is called clustering. See if you can name the category of each cluster of sticky notes. If one cluster becomes very large, think how you can split it into two or more smaller clusters.

If you are not sure how to group the sticky notes into clusters, try asking yourself the What? Where? When? Why? Who? and How? Questions.

As you read the text and think about where new topics may fit in, you will find that the topic starts to take more form in your mind.

TIP: Use a 'parking space' where you place sticky notes that you do not know where to place temporarily. Make sure by the end, all sticky notes are in clusters.

Once you are done with the sticky notes, you are ready to put these clusters in a mind map.

Steps of Mind Mapping:

Step 1: Write a **central idea** in a circle or draw an image on the middle of a blank sheet.

TIP: we recommend you use a pencil for the first draft of the mind map, so you can change things as you go along. Later on, you will fill in the branches and sub-branches with colors and images.

Step 2: Draw **thick branches** out from the center word or image. The number of branches depends on the number of clusters you created with the sticky notes. Each cluster will be one branch.

Step 3: Write one keyword on each branch: the word for the category of that cluster.

TIP: you can use CAPS for the main branches and lower-case letters for the sub-branches

Step 4: From every one of these main branches, draw **thinner branches**, like in a tree. Each of these thinner branches is a sub-topic. Write a key word on each of these thinner branches. You can continue splitting up branches into smaller branches as much as you need to show the information.

However, usually mind maps do not go beyond the third level as it will become very cluttered. Remember, the topics of the sub-branches should be included in the topic of the main branches.

Step 5: Use a different color for each main branch (and its sub-branches) to help you organize the clusters. Use images or symbols to help your remember the topics more vividly.

TIP: Use a parking list on the side, for topics that are unclear where they fit in the mind map. You can always add these later. Sometimes, having several ideas in a parking list means you may have to research the topic a bit more.

Clouds:

Sometimes, ideas are truly related to the main topic, but do not find a place on the branches. It is possible to put them in their own bubble or cloud in the margins of the mind map, without any connections to the branches. However, having many clouds in your map, might mean that you have to research your topic a bit more.

Works of Art

Some mind maps are truly works of art, with many drawings and images embedded in the map. Once you have sketched out your basic mind map, take your time to add colors and images.

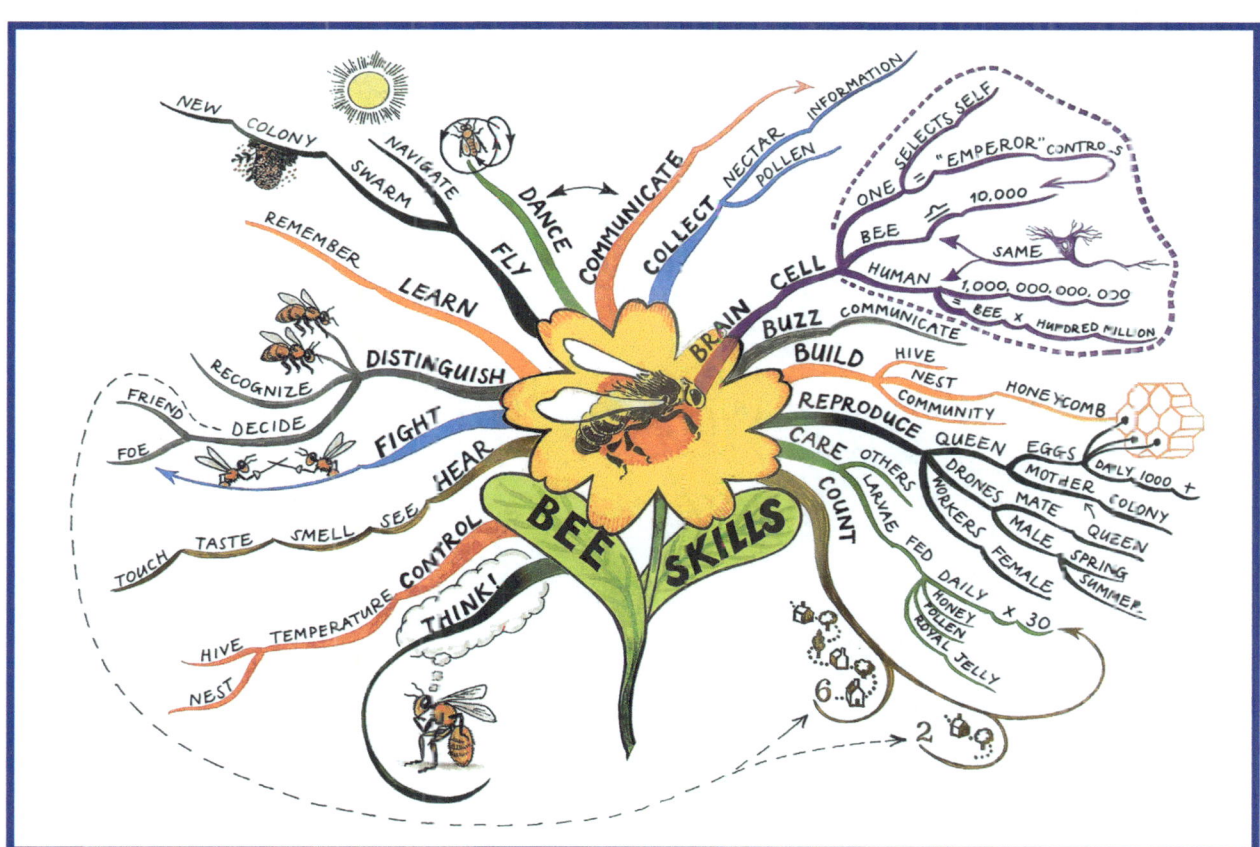

When you mind map, we want you to take your time. First you organize your information with sticky notes. Then, you will sketch your mind map. Lastly, make your mind map look pretty: use colors and images.

Use both the time slots for the Skill and the Project to work on one mind map, so make it something amazing!

Did you know: Mind Mapping is a really cool skill you can use to understand, organize or plan anything? Check out the map below on planning family events.

Your Turn:
As you read, use sticky notes to make clusters of important points. Think of a name for each cluster.

- Sketch the central idea and the main branches.
- Add on level of sub-branches with sub-topics.
- Use key words on each branch
- Use colors.
- **Add images.**

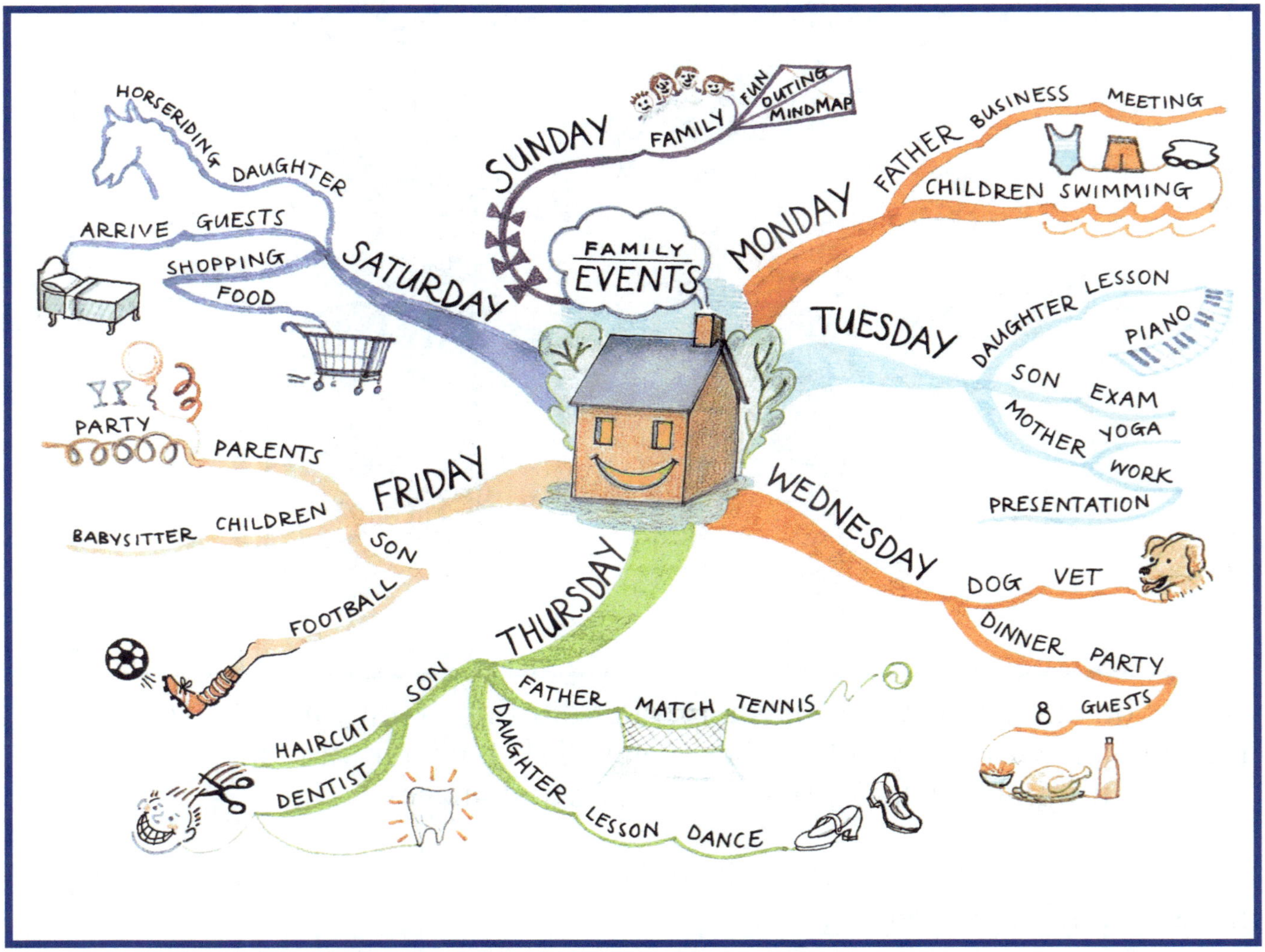

From The Ultimate Book of Mind Mapping by Tony Buzan

MAP:

Trace the map for Ancient Africa: which map do you need? Where can you find this area on the World Wall Map?

Mark in your map the following:
- Label the seas & oceans
- Trace the Nile river
- Trace the Niger river
- Shade the area of the Sahara Desert
- Mark Egypt
- Mark the kingdom of Kush
- Mark the kingdom of Axum
- Mark where the people of Nok used to live

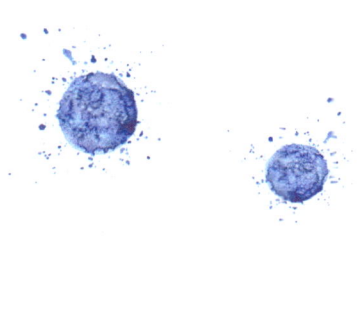

Use the map in the encyclopedia to help you.

Make sure your map is labeled correctly.

TIMELINE:

Add Ancient Africa to your timeline.

Use the box with dates in the encyclopedia to add more events to your timeline.

Remember to pay attention to location.

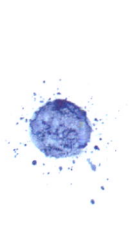

WEEK: 25	INDIA		
KEYWORDS:	Aryan people, Mauryan Empire, Gupta Empire, Caste System, Buddhism	**RESOURCES:**	UILE
SKILL:	Mind Map	**PROJECT:**	Mind Map
MAPPING:	India	**TIMELINING:**	India

EXPLANATION

TOPIC: INDIA

Remember the people of the Indus valley? And the mysterious disappearance of the Mohenjo-Daro people? Eventually, the people that settled in this area were called Aryans, And after a while, they spread out across all of India. India is known for its many gods and religions. The main religion is Hinduism, which started with the Aryan priests. The early Aryans divided people into different groups according to their job. The children of such people would automatically belong to the same group and do the same job. This is known as the Caste System. Once you are born into a certain group, you cannot change and be part of another group.

RESEARCH:

You know what to do!

Find your resources, and read the text. Use the check-list below and the **cheat sheet** to ask yourself the questions.

Check-list:

- Find your resources
- Ask yourself the questions before reading
- Write down difficult words
- Read the text
- Ask yourself the questions during reading
- Ask yourself the questions after reading
- Check in with yourself
- Form your opinion

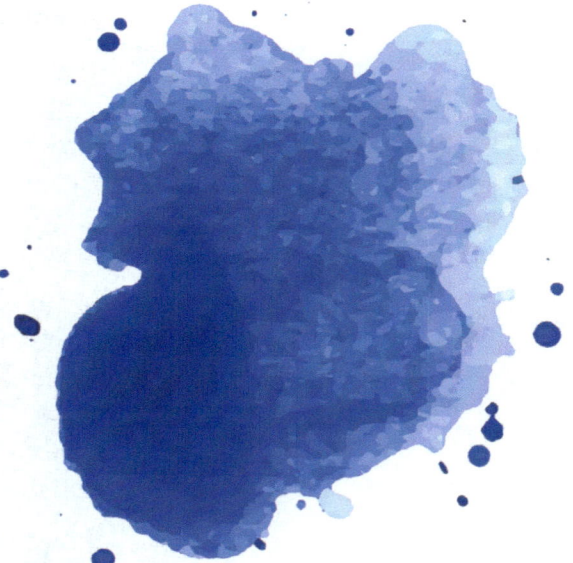

Mind mapping means you make a map of thoughts or pieces of information. Mind maps help you understand, organize and memorize information. They help you get an overview on more complex ideas and they can stimulate your creativity. Mind maps help students save time studying and help prepare for exams. Because the mind map forces you to think radially, you often uncover wider and more interesting ideas.

Before you mind map:

Since we use mind maps to organize and understand information from a text, we start by looking at that information. Get a stack of sticky notes. As you read the text, write down the important ideas in one word on the sticky notes: one idea per sticky note. Now briefly summarize the idea under the word.

Stick your sticky notes on the wall (or a door, window, desk etc). Group similar main points together, this is called clustering. See if you can name the category of each cluster of sticky notes. If one cluster becomes very large, think how you can split it into two or more smaller clusters.

If you are not sure how to group the sticky notes into clusters, try asking yourself the What? Where? When? Why? Who? and How? Questions.

As you read the text and think about where new topics may fit in, you will find that the topic starts to take more form in your mind.

TIP: Use a 'parking space' where you place sticky notes that you do not know where to place temporarily. Make sure by the end, all sticky notes are in clusters.

Once you are done with the sticky notes, you are ready to put these clusters in a mind map.

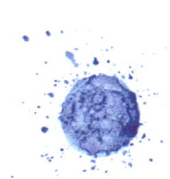

Steps of Mind Mapping:

Step 1: Write a **central idea** in a circle or draw an image on the middle of a blank sheet.

TIP: we recommend you use a pencil for the first draft of the mind map, so you can change things as you go along. Later on, you will fill in the branches and sub-branches with colors and images.

Step 2: Draw **thick branches** out from the center word or image. The number of branches depends on the number of clusters you created with the sticky notes. Each cluster will be one branch.

Step 3: Write one keyword on each branch: the word for the category of that cluster.

TIP: you can use CAPS for the main branches and lower-case letters for the sub-branches

Step 4: From every one of these main branches, draw **thinner branches**, like in a tree. Each of these thinner branches is a sub-topic. Write a key word on each of these thinner branches. You can continue splitting up branches into smaller branches as much as you need to show the information.

However, usually mind maps do not go beyond the third level as it will become very cluttered. Remember, the topics of the sub-branches should be included in the topic of the main branches.

Step 5: Use a different color for each main branch (and its sub-branches) to help you organize the clusters. Use images or symbols to help your remember the topics more vividly.

TIP: Use a parking list on the side, for topics that are unclear where they fit in the mind map. You can always add these later. Sometimes, having several ideas in a parking list means you may have to research the topic a bit more.

Clouds:

Sometimes, ideas are truly related to the main topic, but do not find a place on the branches. It is possible to put them in their own bubble or cloud in the margins of the mind map, without any connections to the branches. However, having many clouds in your map, might mean that you have to research your topic a bit more.

Works of Art

Some mind maps are truly works of art, with many drawings and images embedded in the map. Once you have sketched out your basic mind map, take your time to add colors and images.

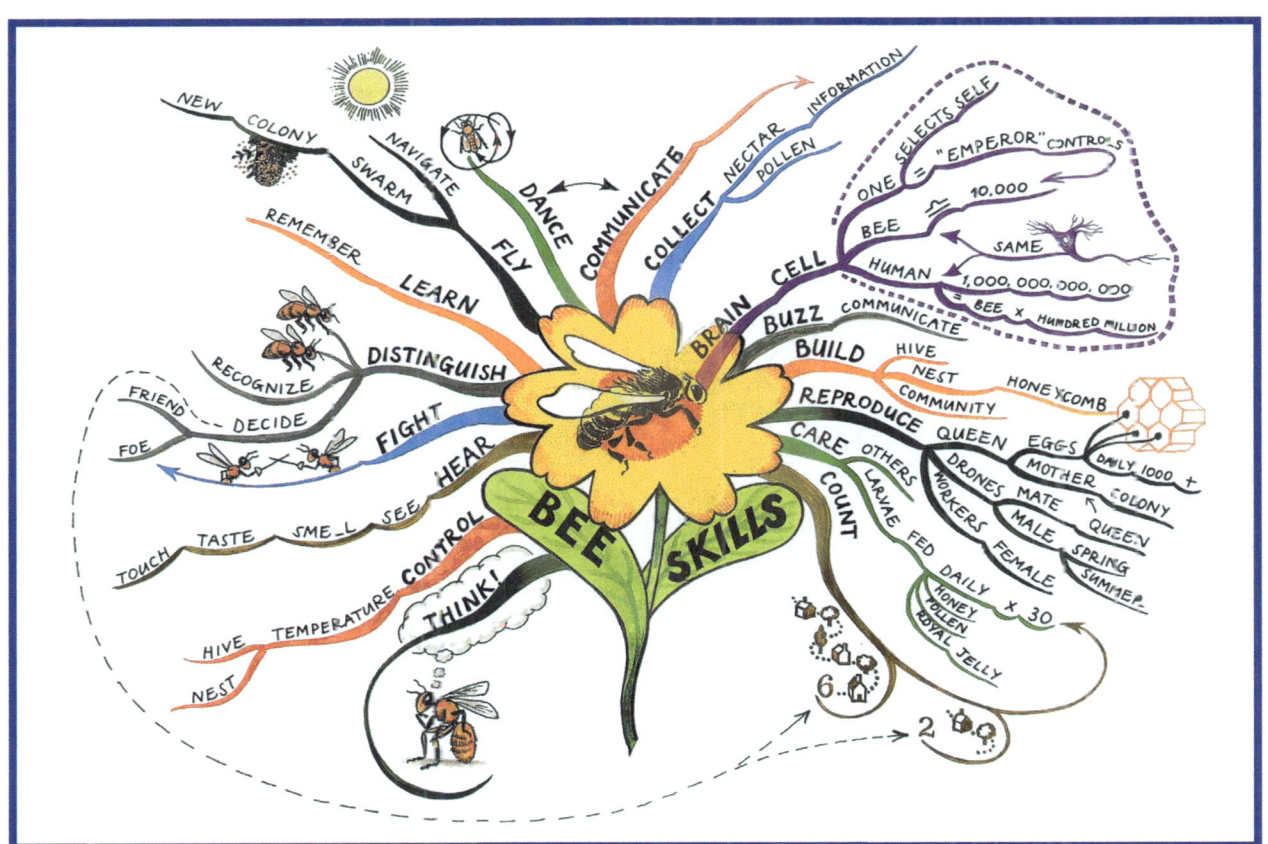

When you mind map, we want you to take your time. First you organize your information with sticky notes. Then, you will sketch your mind map. Lastly, make your mind map look pretty: use colors and images.

Use both the time slots for the Skill and the Project to work on one mind map, so make it something amazing!

SKILL & PROJECT:

Your Turn:

As you read, use sticky notes to make clusters of important points. Think of a name for each cluster.

- Sketch the central idea and the main branches.
- Add on level of sub-branches with sub-topics.
- Use key words on each branch
- Use colors.
- Add images.

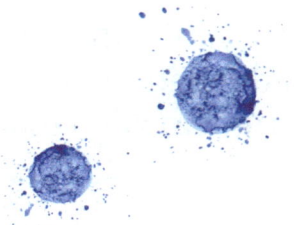

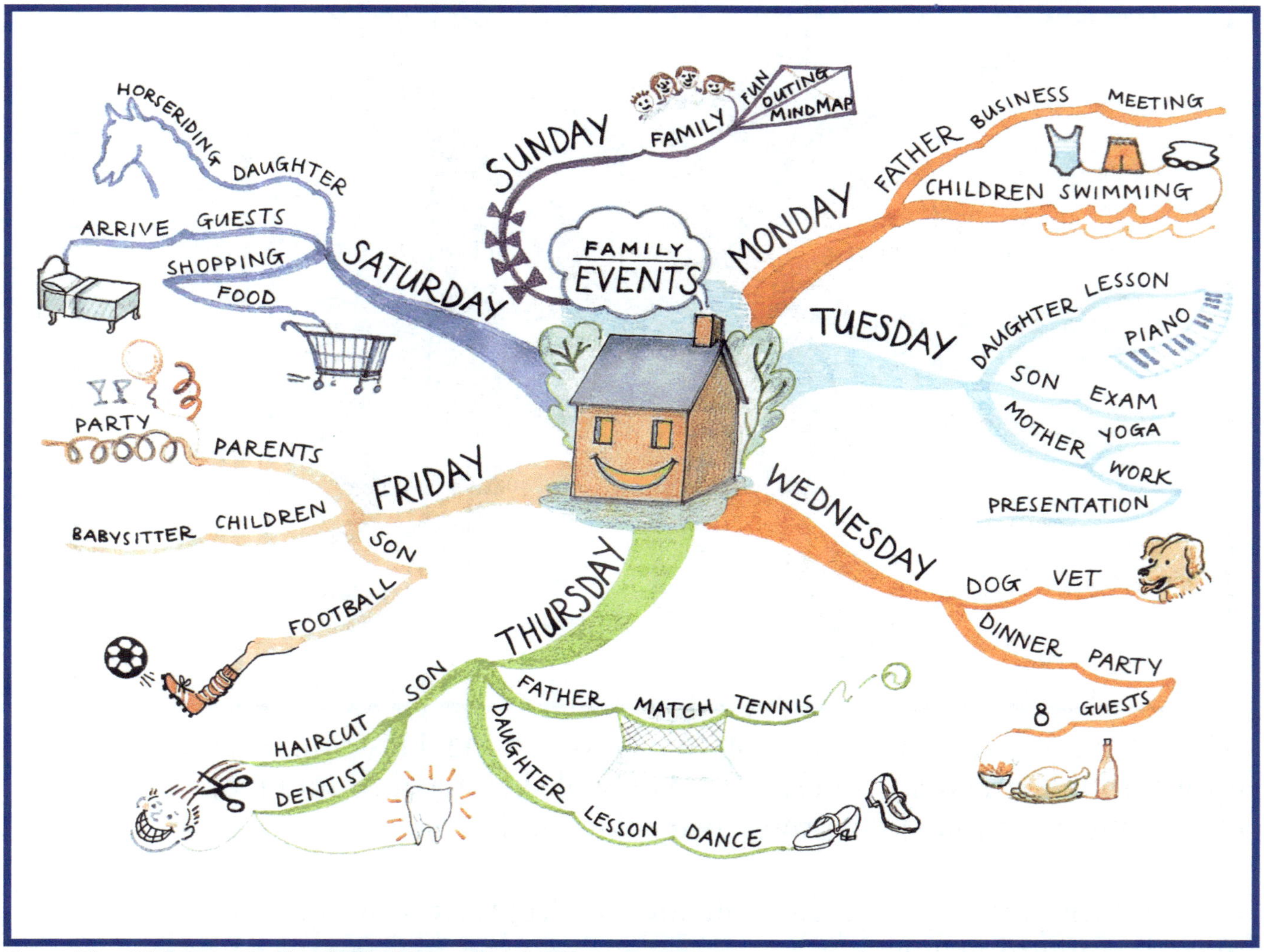

From The Ultimate Book of Mind Mapping by Tony Buzan

MAP:

Trace the map for Ancient India: which map do you need? Where can you find this area on the World Wall Map?

Mark in your map the following:
- Label the seas & oceans
- Trace the Indus river
- Trace the Ganges river
- Shade the area of the Mauryan Empire

Use the map in the encyclopedia to help you.

Make sure your map is labeled correctly.

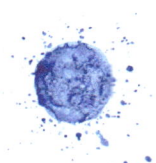

TIMELINE:

Add Ancient India to your timeline.

Use the box with dates in the encyclopedia to add more events to your timeline.

Remember to pay attention to location.

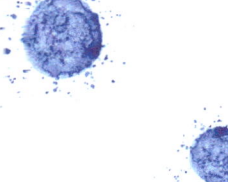

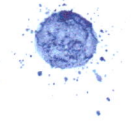

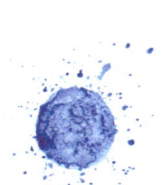

WEEK: 26   **ARABIA**

KEYWORDS: Sabaa kingdom, Nabataea kingdom, Petra   **RESOURCES:**   UILE
HI

SKILL: Mind Map   **PROJECT:**   Mind Map

MAPPING: Arabia   **TIMELINING:**   Arabia

EXPLANATION

TOPIC: ARABIA

We have already learned a lot about Arabia: Prophet Ibrahim (as) left his wife Hajar and baby Ismaeel in the desert, when there was no Makkah yet. Prophet Musa (as) crossed the sea and wandered in the deserts of Arabia for 40 years. When we read the story of prophet Sulayman (as), we learned about the queen of Sheba, whose kingdom was located in the south part of Arabia. In Sheba there was more rain and so they had more plants and gardens.

The rest of Arabia was desert. Many of the early people in Arabia were nomads, as there was no water for the people, animals and plants. So they would wander around, from one watering hole to another. In order to keep moving, they lived in tents: they could be easily packed up when they needed to move to another watering hole.

Arabia was very special among the ancient civilizations. Not only because most of the prophets lived there, but they were also special because they had many languages very early on. And even more amazing was that the nomads could read and write and left many written texts for us. This helps us a great deal to know more about the people who lived in ancient Arabia. Still, we do not know where the Arabs really came from. Arabia lay between Egypt and Mesopotamia.

RESEARCH:

You know what to do!

Find your resources, and read the text. Use the check-list below and the **cheat sheet** to ask yourself the questions.

Check-list:

- Find your resources
- Ask yourself the questions before reading
- Write down difficult words
- Read the text
- Ask yourself the questions during reading
- Ask yourself the questions after reading
- Check in with yourself
- Form your opinion

SKILL & PROJECT:

Mind mapping means you make a map of thoughts or pieces of information.

Before you mind map:

Since we use mind maps to organize and understand information from a text, we start by looking at that information. Get a stack of sticky notes. As you read the text, write down the important ideas in one word on the sticky notes: one idea per sticky note. Now briefly summarize the idea under the word.

Stick your sticky notes on the wall (or a door, window, desk etc). Group similar main points together, this is called clustering. See if you can name the category of each cluster of sticky notes. If one cluster becomes very large, think how you can split it into two or more smaller clusters.

If you are not sure how to group the sticky notes into clusters, try asking yourself the What? Where? When? Why? Who? and How? Questions.

As you read the text and think about where new topics may fit in, you will find that the topic starts to take more form in your mind.

TIP: Use a 'parking space' where you place sticky notes that you do not know where to place temporarily. Make sure by the end, all sticky notes are in clusters.

Once you are done with the sticky notes, you are ready to put these clusters in a mind map.

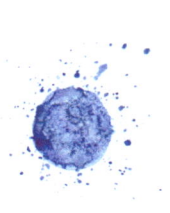

Steps of Mind Mapping:

Step 1: Write a **central idea** in a circle or draw an image on the middle of a blank sheet.

TIP: we recommend you use a pencil for the first draft of the mind map, so you can change things as you go along. Later on, you will fill in the branches and sub-branches with colors and images.

Step 2: Draw **thick branches** out from the center word or image. The number of branches depends on the number of clusters you created with the sticky notes. Each cluster will be one branch.

Step 3: Write one keyword on each branch: the word for the category of that cluster.

TIP: you can use CAPS for the main branches and lower-case letters for the sub-branches

Step 4: From every one of these main branches, draw **thinner branches**, like in a tree. Each of these thinner branches is a sub-topic. Write a key word on each of these thinner branches. You can continue splitting up branches into smaller branches as much as you need to show the information.

However, usually mind maps do not go beyond the third level as it will become very cluttered. Remember, the topics of the sub-branches should be included in the topic of the main branches.

Step 5: Use a different color for each main branch (and its sub-branches) to help you organize the clusters. Use images or symbols to help your remember the topics more vividly.

TIP: Use a parking list on the side, for topics that are unclear where they fit in the mind map. You can always add these later. Sometimes, having several ideas in a parking list means you may have to research the topic a bit more.

Clouds:

Sometimes, ideas are truly related to the main topic, but do not find a place on the branches. It is possible to put them in their own bubble or cloud in the margins of the mind map, without any connections to the branches. However, having many clouds in your map, might mean that you have to research your topic a bit more.

Works of Art

Some mind maps are truly works of art, with many drawings and images embedded in the map. Once you have sketched out your basic mind map, take your time to add colors and images.

When you mind map, we want you to take your time. First you organize your information with sticky notes. Then, you will sketch your mind map. Lastly, make your mind map look pretty: use colors and images.

Use both the time slots for the Skill and the Project to work on one mind map, so make it something amazing!

Your Turn:

As you read, use sticky notes to make clusters of important points. Think of a name for each cluster.

- Sketch the central idea and the main branches.
- Add on level of sub-branches with sub-topics.
- Use key words on each branch
- Use colors.
- Add images.

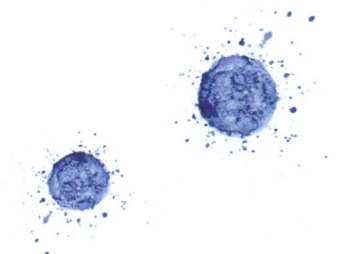

From The Ultimate Book of Mind Mapping by Tony Buzan

MAP:

Trace the map for Ancient Arabia: which map do you need? Where can you find this area on the World Wall Map?

Mark in your map the following:
- Label the seas & oceans
- Mark Nabataea
- Mark Sabae
- Mark Petra
- Draw an arrow from the south side of Arabia up to Petra, then to the Mediterranean Sea to show the trading routes.

Use the map in the encyclopedia to help you.

Make sure your map is labeled correctly.

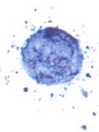

TIMELINE:

Add Ancient Arabia to your timeline.

Use the box with dates in the encyclopedia and the information from the History Intersections to add more events to your timeline.

Remember to pay attention to location.

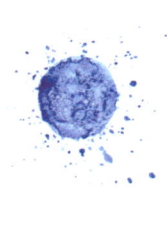

WEEK: 27	NATIVE AMERICANS		
KEYWORDS:	Adena, Hopewell, Maya, Olmecs, Nazca	RESOURCES:	UILE
SKILL:	Mind Map	PROJECT:	Mind Map
MAPPING:	America	TIMELINING:	America

EXPLANATION

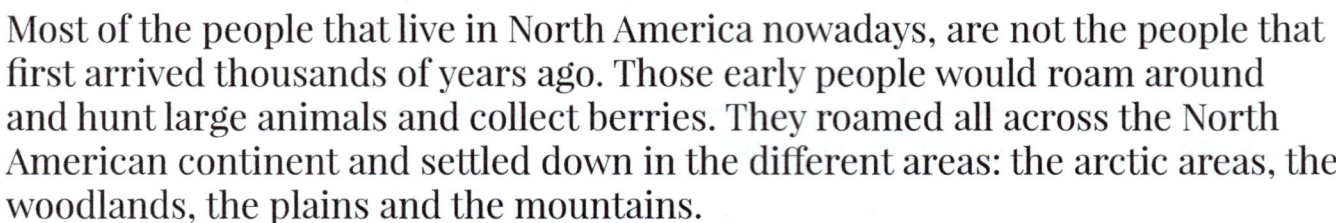

TOPIC: NATIVE AMERICANS

Most of the people that live in North America nowadays, are not the people that first arrived thousands of years ago. Those early people would roam around and hunt large animals and collect berries. They roamed all across the North American continent and settled down in the different areas: the arctic areas, the woodlands, the plains and the mountains.

RESEARCH:

You know what to do!

Find your resources, and read the text. Use the check-list below and the **cheat sheet** to ask yourself the questions.

Check-list:

- Find your resources
- Ask yourself the questions before reading
- Write down difficult words
- Read the text
- Ask yourself the questions during reading
- Ask yourself the questions after reading
- Check in with yourself
- Form your opinion

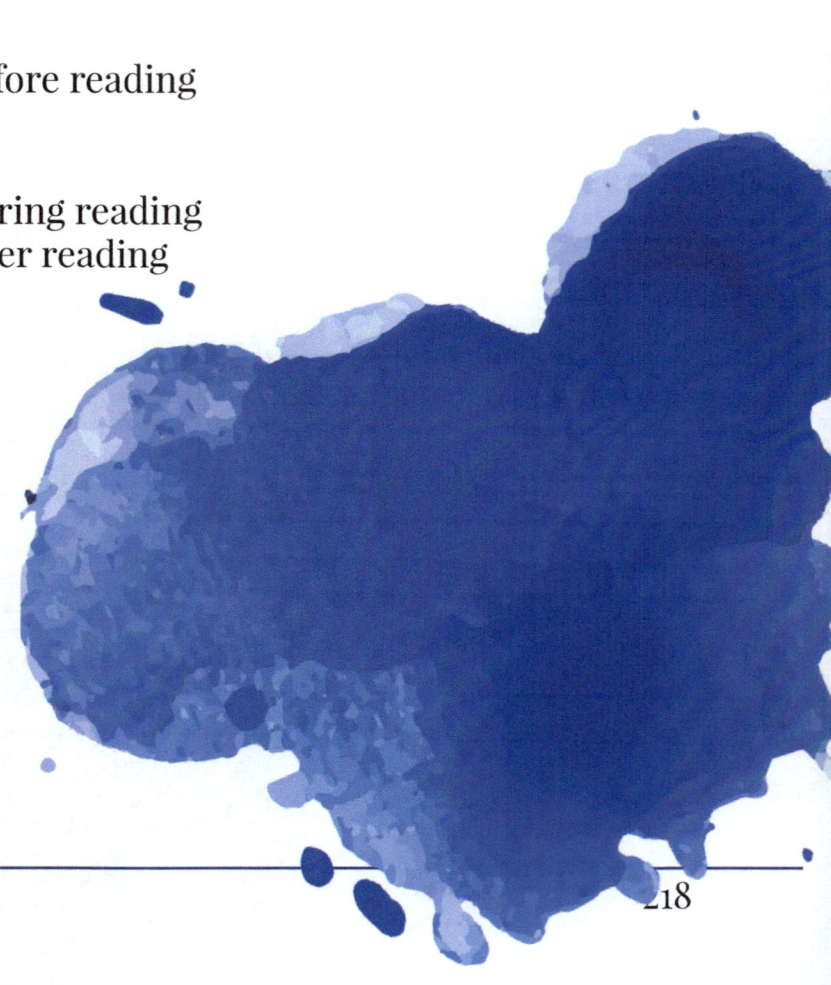

Mind mapping means you make a map of thoughts or pieces of information.

Before you mind map:

Since we use mind maps to organize and understand information from a text, we start by looking at that information. Get a stack of sticky notes. As you read the text, write down the important ideas in one word on the sticky notes: one idea per sticky note. Now briefly summarize the idea under the word.

Stick your sticky notes on the wall (or a door, window, desk etc). Group similar main points together, this is called clustering. See if you can name the category of each cluster of sticky notes. If one cluster becomes very large, think how you can split it into two or more smaller clusters.

If you are not sure how to group the sticky notes into clusters, try asking yourself the What? Where? When? Why? Who? and How? Questions.

As you read the text and think about where new topics may fit in, you will find that the topic starts to take more form in your mind.

TIP: use a 'parking space' where you place sticky notes that you do not know where to place temporarily. Make sure by the end, all sticky notes are in clusters.

Once you are done with the sticky notes, you are ready to put these clusters in a mind map.

Steps of Mind Mapping:

Step 1: Write a **central idea** in a circle or draw an image on the middle of a blank sheet.

Step 2: Draw **thick branches** out from the center word or image. The number of branches depends on the number of clusters you created with the sticky notes. Each cluster will be one branch.

Step 3: Write one keyword on each branch: the word for the category of that cluster.

Step 4: From every one of these main branches, draw **thinner branches**, like in a tree. Each of these thinner branches is a sub-topic. Write a key word on each of these thinner branches. You can continue splitting up branches into smaller branches as much as you need to show the information.

However, usually mind maps do not go beyond the third level as it will become very cluttered. Remember, the topics of the sub-branches should be included in the topic of the main branches.

Step 5: Use a different color for each main branch (and its sub-branches) to help you organize the clusters. Use images or symbols to help your remember the topics more vividly.

TIP: use a parking list on the side, for topics that are unclear where they fit in the mind map. You can always add these later. Sometimes, having several ideas in a parking list means you may have to research the topic a bit more.

Clouds:

Sometimes, ideas are truly related to the main topic, but do not find a place on the branches. It is possible to put them in their own bubble or cloud in the margins of the mind map, without any connections to the branches. However, having many clouds in your map, might mean that you have to research your topic a bit more.

Works of Art

Some mind maps are truly works of art, with many drawings and images embedded in the map. Once you have sketched out your basic mind map, take your time to add colors and images.

When you mind map, we want you to take your time. First you organize your information with sticky notes. Then, you will sketch your mind map. Lastly, make your mind map look pretty: use colors and images.

Use both the time slots for the Skill and the Project to work on one mind map, so make it something amazing!

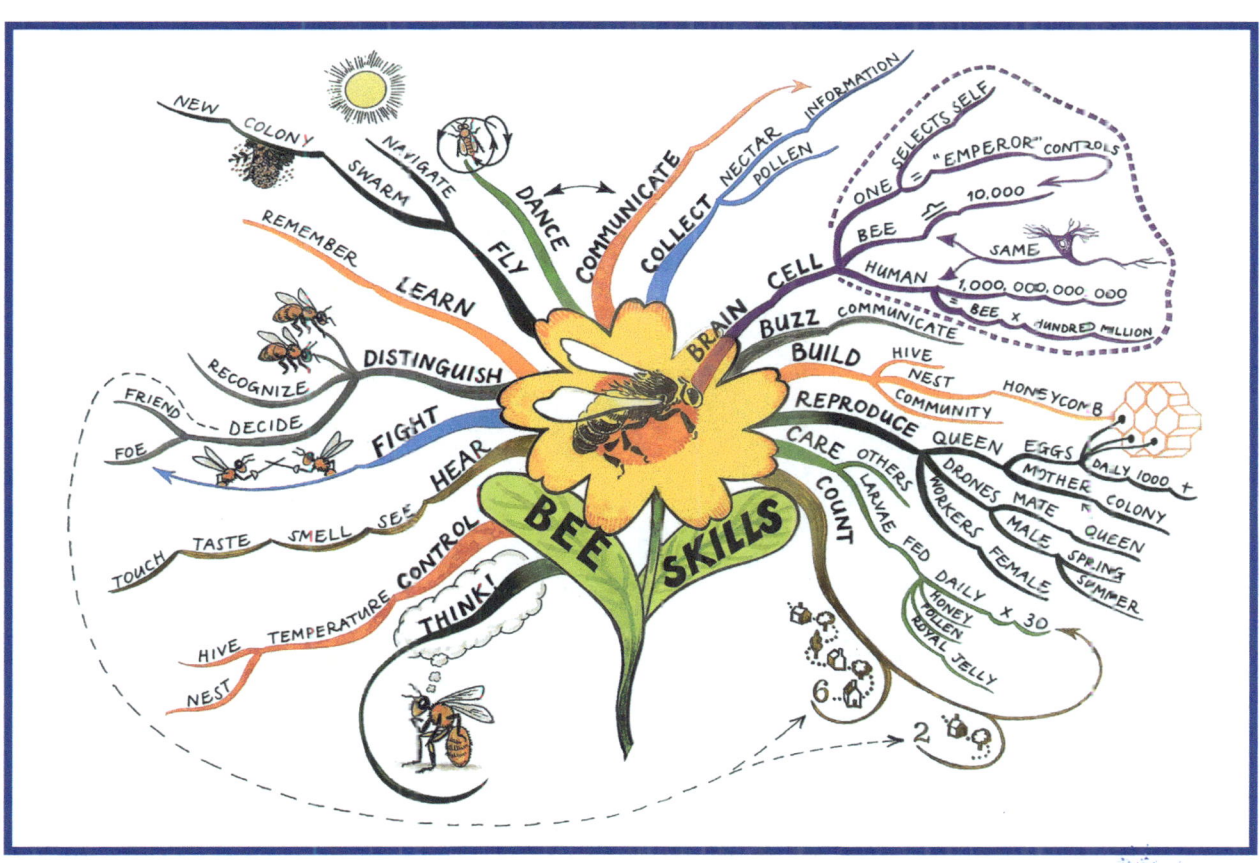

Your Turn:

As you read, use sticky notes to make clusters of important points. Think of a name for each cluster.

- Sketch the central idea and the main branches.
- Add on level of sub-branches with sub-topics.
- Use key words on each branch
- Use colors.
- Add images.

Take your time to truly make your mind map colorful and full with images and symbols

From The Ultimate Book of Mind Mapping by Tony Buzan

MAP:

There were many different tribes in the Americas, in north America, South America and Central America. You will need the text to place the different tribes.

Trace the map for the Americas: which map do you need? Where can you find this area on the World Wall Map?

Mark in your map the following:
- Label the seas & oceans

In North America:
- Mark the Great Plains
- Mark the Adena and Hopewell people

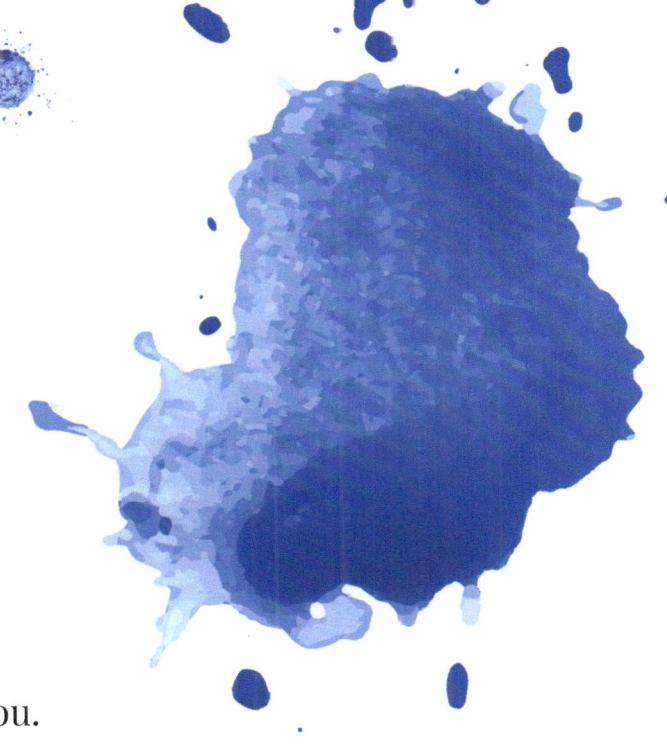

In Central America:
- Mark Teotihuacan
- Shade the land of the Maya people

In South America:
- Mark the Nazca people
- Mark the Moche people

Use the map in the encyclopedia to help you.

Make sure your map is labeled correctly.

TIMELINE:

Add Native Americans to your timeline.

Use the box with dates in the encyclopedia to add more events to your timeline.

Remember to pay attention to location.

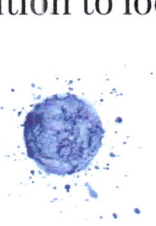

WEEK: 28	**CELTS**		
KEYWORDS:	Gaul, Britain, Ireland	**RESOURCES:**	UILE
SKILL:	Mind Map	**PROJECT:**	Mind Map
MAPPING:	Celts	**TIMELINING:**	Celts

EXPLANATION

TOPIC: CELTS

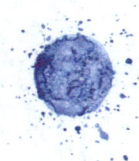

In ancient Europe there were many tribes that were called the Celts. The word Celt comes from the Greek 'keltoi' and means barbarian. During the ancient times, these ancient people were not called Celts, and they did not call themselves this way. This name was given to them much later. The Romans used to call them the 'Britons'. The Celts were divided into three groups: the Gauls, the Gales and the Britons. Historians grouped them together as Celts because they had a similar way of life and a similar language.

When the Roman Empire kept growing, they slowly took over all the land of the Celts. Eventually, only in Ireland, Scotland and Wales did the Celtic way of life survive.

RESEARCH:

You know what to do!

Find your resources, and read the text. Use the check-list below and the **cheat sheet** to ask yourself the questions.

Check-list:

- Find your resources
- Ask yourself the questions before reading
- Write down difficult words
- Read the text
- Ask yourself the questions during reading
- Ask yourself the questions after reading
- Check in with yourself
- Form your opinion

Mind mapping means you make a map of thoughts or pieces of information.

Before you mind map:

Since we use mind maps to organize and understand information from a text, we start by looking at that information. Get a stack of sticky notes. As you read the text, write down the important ideas in one word on the sticky notes: one idea per sticky note. Now briefly summarize the idea under the word.

Stick your sticky notes on the wall (or a door, window, desk etc). Group similar main points together, this is called clustering. See if you can name the category of each cluster of sticky notes. If one cluster becomes very large, think how you can split it into two or more smaller clusters.

If you are not sure how to group the sticky notes into clusters, try asking yourself the What? Where? When? Why? Who? and How? Questions.

As you read the text and think about where new topics may fit in, you will find that the topic starts to take more form in your mind.

TIP: use a 'parking space' where you place sticky notes that you do not know where to place temporarily. Make sure by the end, all sticky notes are in clusters.

Once you are done with the sticky notes, you are ready to put these clusters in a mind map.

Steps of Mind Mapping:

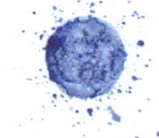

Step 1: Write a **central idea** in a circle or draw an image on the middle of a blank sheet.

Step 2: Draw **thick branches** out from the center word or image. The number of branches depends on the number of clusters you created with the sticky notes. Each cluster will be one branch.

Step 3: Write one keyword on each branch: the word for the category of that cluster.

Step 4: From every one of these main branches, draw **thinner branches**, like in a tree. Each of these thinner branches is a sub-topic. Write a key word on each of these thinner branches. You can continue splitting up branches into smaller branches as much as you need to show the information.

However, usually mind maps do not go beyond the third level as it will become very cluttered. Remember, the topics of the sub-branches should be included in the topic of the main branches.

Step 5: Use a different color for each main branch (and its sub-branches) to help you organize the clusters. Use images or symbols to help your remember the topics more vividly.

Clouds:

Sometimes, ideas are truly related to the main topic, but do not find a place on the branches. It is possible to put them in their own bubble or cloud in the margins of the mind map, without any connections to the branches. However, having many clouds in your map, might mean that you have to research your topic a bit more.

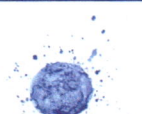

Works of Art

Some mind maps are truly works of art, with many drawings and images embedded in the map. Once you have sketched out your basic mind map, take your time to add colors and images.

When you mind map, we want you to take your time. First you organize your information with sticky notes. Then, you will sketch your mind map. Lastly, make your mind map look pretty: use colors and images.

Use both the time slots for the Skill and the Project to work on one mind map, so make it something amazing!

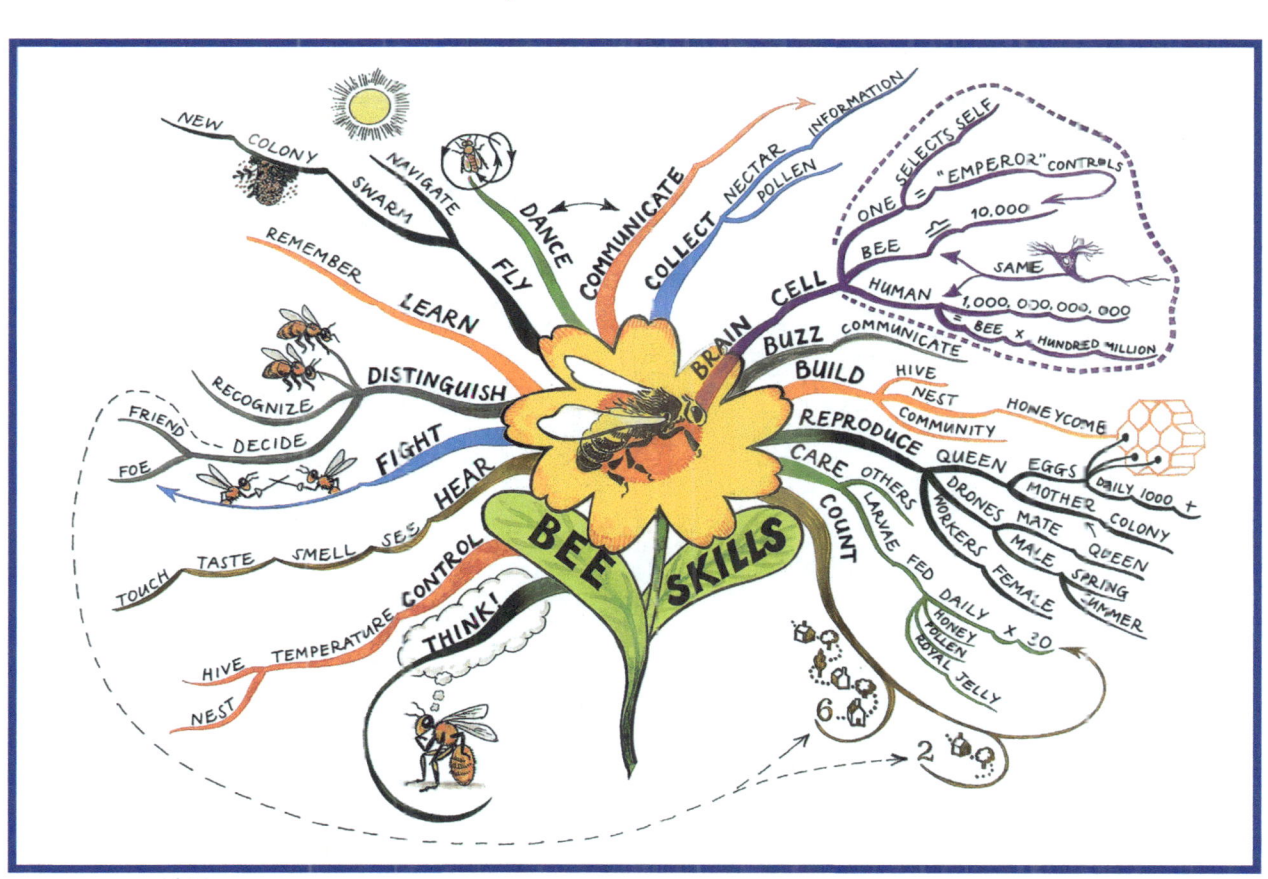

Your Turn:

As you read, use sticky notes to make clusters of important points. Think of a name for each cluster.

- Sketch the central idea and the main branches.
- Add on level of sub-branches with sub-topics.
- Use key words on each branch
- Use colors.
- Add images.

Take your time to truly make your mind map colorful and full with images and symbols

From The Ultimate Book of Mind Mapping by Tony Buzan

MAP:

Trace the map for the Celts: which map do you need? Where can you find this area on the World Wall Map?

Mark in your map the following:
- Label the seas & oceans
- Mark Ireland
- Mark Britain
- Mark Asia Minor
- Mark the area of the homeland of the Celts with a dark color
- Shade the area where they spread.

Use the map in the encyclopedia to help you.

Make sure your map is labeled correctly.

TIMELINE:

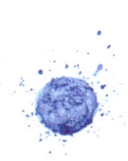

Add the Celts to your timeline.

Use the box with dates in the encyclopedia and the information from the History Intersections to add more events to your timeline.

Remember to pay attention to location.

WEEK: 29	ROME		
KEYWORDS:	Romulus, Senate, Punic Wars, Julius Ceasar, Aqueducts	RESOURCES:	UILE
SKILL:	Choice	PROJECT:	Diagramming
MAPPING:	Roman Empire	TIMELINING:	Romans

EXPLANATION

TOPIC: ROME

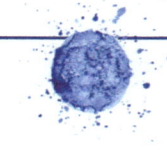

The history of Rome is divided into three parts: the beginning as a Kingdom, then the Republic and then the Roman Empire.

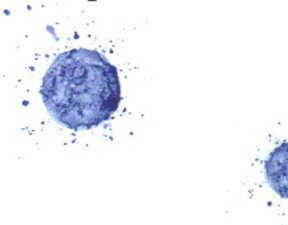

RESEARCH:

You know what to do!

Find your resources, and read the text. Use the check-list below and the **cheat sheet** to ask yourself the questions.

Check-list:

- Find your resources
- Ask yourself the questions before reading
- Write down difficult words
- Read the text
- Ask yourself the questions during reading
- Ask yourself the questions after reading
- Check in with yourself
- Form your opinion

SKILL: CHOICE

We have practiced several skills throughout the year. Today, pick the one that you liked the best and use it to write down the information you have researched.

To remind you, we have covered:

> I. Outlining
> > a. basic level
> > b. secondary level
>
> II. Note taking
> III. Summarizing
> IV. Mind Mapping

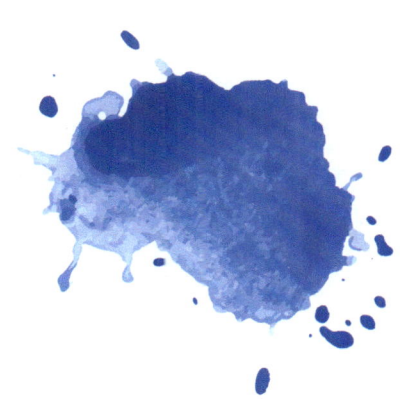

Show us what you got!

PROJECT: DIAGRAMMING

Remember how making diagram means you show information in a visual form? We will do another diagram this week.

5 Easy Steps to make a diagram:

Step 1: Look at what information you have: how does it relate to each other?
Step 2: Look at the diagrams: what relationship does each diagram show?
Step 3: Choose a diagram that fits your information
Step 4: Draw the diagram
Step 5: Add the information in the diagram

All parts of the diagram need to be labeled. Your drawing does not need to be perfect, but needs to show the problem and your thought process.

Your Turn:

Diagram the three time periods of the Romans. Make sure you choose a diagram that allows you to list the three periods, with space to write details for each.

Remember the 5 steps above to guide you in making your diagram. Use the image on the other page to help you choose.

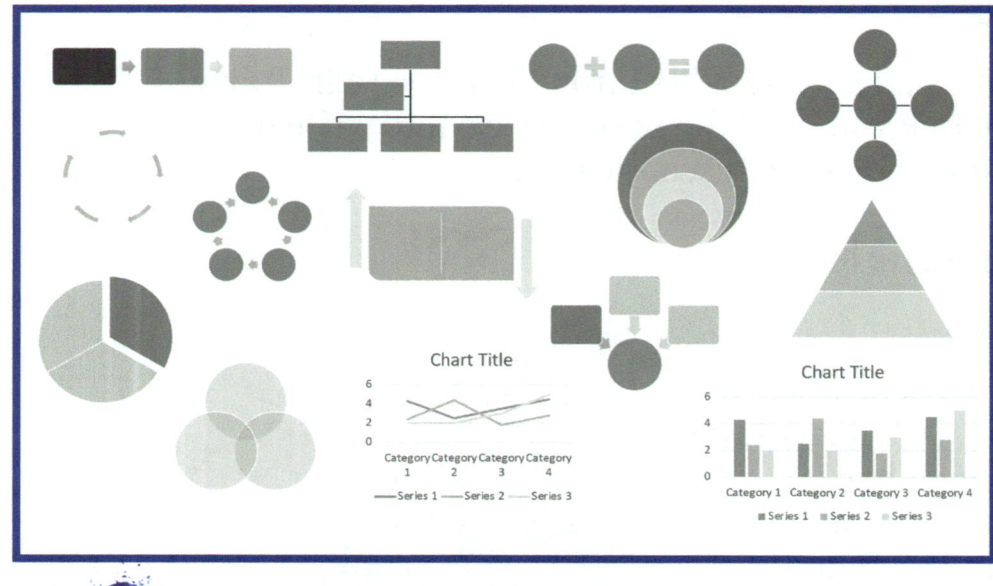

MAP:

Trace the map for the Roman Empire: which map do you need? Where can you find this area on the World Wall Map?

Mark in your map the following:
- Label the seas & oceans
- Mark Rome
- Mark Carthage
- Shade the area of the Roman Empire at its peak.

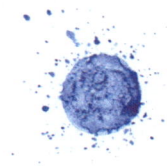

Use the map in the encyclopedia to help you.

Make sure your map is labeled correctly.

TIMELINE:

Add the Romans to your timeline.

Use the box with dates in the encyclopedia to add more events to your timeline.

Remember to pay attention to location.

WEEK: 30	PROPHET ZACHARIAH (AS), PROPHET YAHYA (AS) & PROPHET 'ISA (AS)		
KEYWORDS:	Bethlehem, Nazareth, Jerusalem, Prophet Zachariah (as), Prophet Yahya (as), Prophet 'Isa (as)	RESOURCES:	HI
SKILL:	Choice	PROJECT:	Choice
MAPPING:	Prophet 'Isa (as)	TIMELINING:	Prophet 'Isa (as)

EXPLANATION

TOPIC: **PROPHET ZACHARIAH (AS), PROPHET YAHYA (AS) & PROPHET 'ISA (AS)**

Prophet Zachariah (as) lived at the end of the Ptolemaic Dynasty in Egypt. The Ptolemaic Empire covered Palestine as well. The last of the Ptolemaic rulers was queen Cleopatra, who committed suicide when Egypt fell to Rome. After this, all of the Ptolemaic Empire (including Egypt) became a Roman province.

In Palestine, the Ptolemaic rulers treated the Israelites well. They respected them and let them practice their religion in peace. Prophet 'Isa (as) was born right after the fall of the Ptolemaic Empire, and when the Roman Empire was greatly expanding.

RESEARCH:

You know what to do!

Find your resources, and read the text. Use the check-list below and the **cheat sheet** to ask yourself the questions.

Check-list:

- Find your resources
- Ask yourself the questions before reading
- Write down difficult words
- Read the text
- Ask yourself the question during reading
- Ask yourself the questions after reading
- Check in with yourself
- Form your opinion

SKILL: CHOICE

We have practiced several skills throughout the year. Today, pick the one that you liked the best and use it to write down the information you have researched.

To remind you, we have covered:

> I. Outlining
> > a. basic level
> > b. secondary level
> II. Note taking
> III. Summarizing
> IV. Mind Mapping

Show us what you got!

PROJECT: CHOICE

NEW!

So far, we have covered how to create posters, how to put information in diagrams, how to produce good PowerPoint presentations, and how to make beautiful mind maps. We are sure you have a preference, so pick one of these methods to create something visually stunning.

Show off you skills!

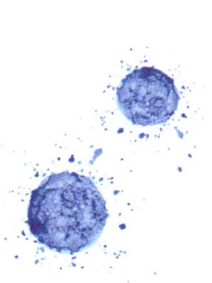

MAP:

Trace the map for Prophet 'Isa (as): which map do you need? Where can you find this area on the World Wall Map?

Mark in your map the following:
- Label the seas & oceans
- Mark Bethlehem
- Mark Nazareth
- Mark Jerusalem
- Mark Egypt
- Draw an arrow from Bethlehem to Jerusalem
- Draw an arrow from Jerusalem to Egypt (to the Nile delta)
- Draw an arrow back from Egypt to Nazareth.

Use the map on the next page to help you.

Make sure your map is labeled correctly.

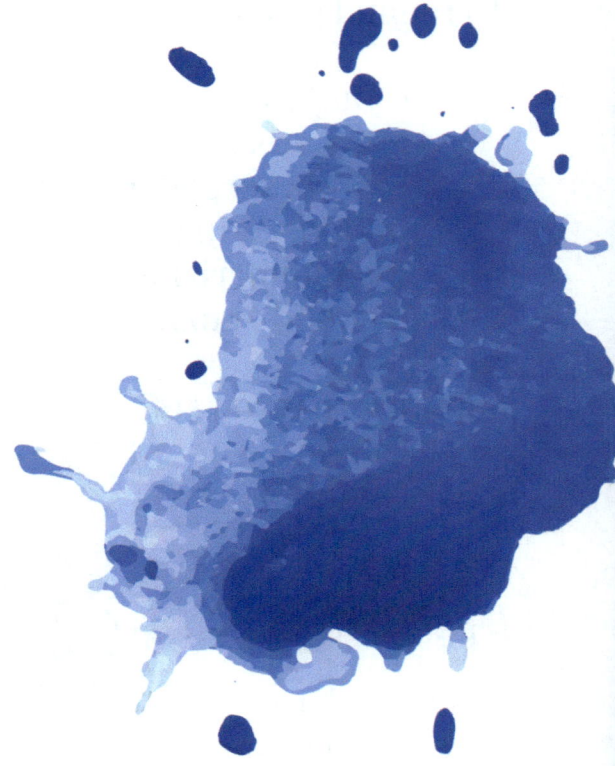

TIMELINE:

Add prophet Zachariah (as), prophet Yahya (as), and prophet 'Isa (as) to your timeline.

Look in the History Intersections, 2nd edition, and see if you can add any other events from this period to your timeline.

Remember to pay attention to location.

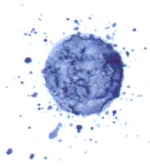

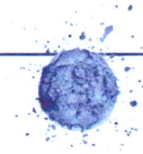

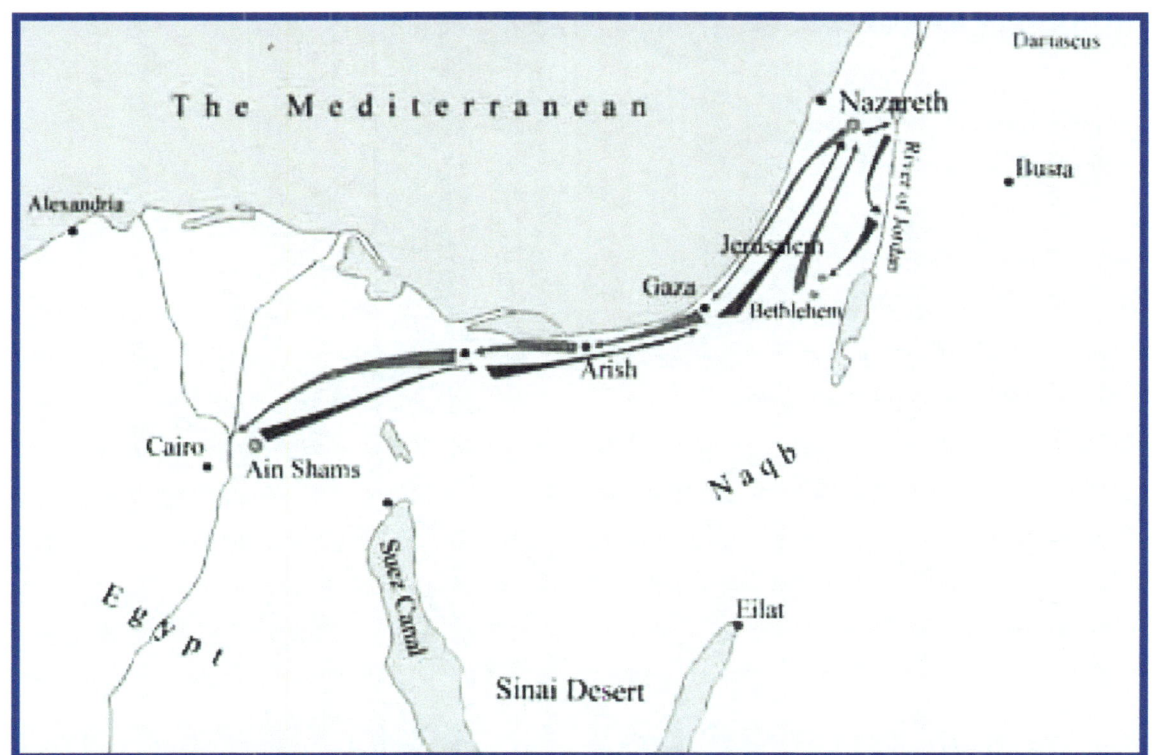

The Mediterranean

Alexandria
Cairo
Ain Shams
Egypt
Suez Canal
Sinai Desert
Arish
Gaza
Jerusalem
Bethlehem
Nazareth
River of Jordan
Damascus
Busra
Naqb
Eilat

APPENDIX

Roman Numerals

Number	Roman Numeral	Number	Roman Numeral
1	I	50	L
2	II	100	C
3	III	500	D
4	IV	1000	M
5	V		
6	VI		
7	VII	So...	
8	VIII	40	XL
9	IX	60	LX
10	X	90	XC
11	XI		
12	XII		
13	XIII		
14	XIV		
15	XV		
16	XVI		
17	XVII		
18	XVIII		
19	XIX		
20	XX		

Color Wheel

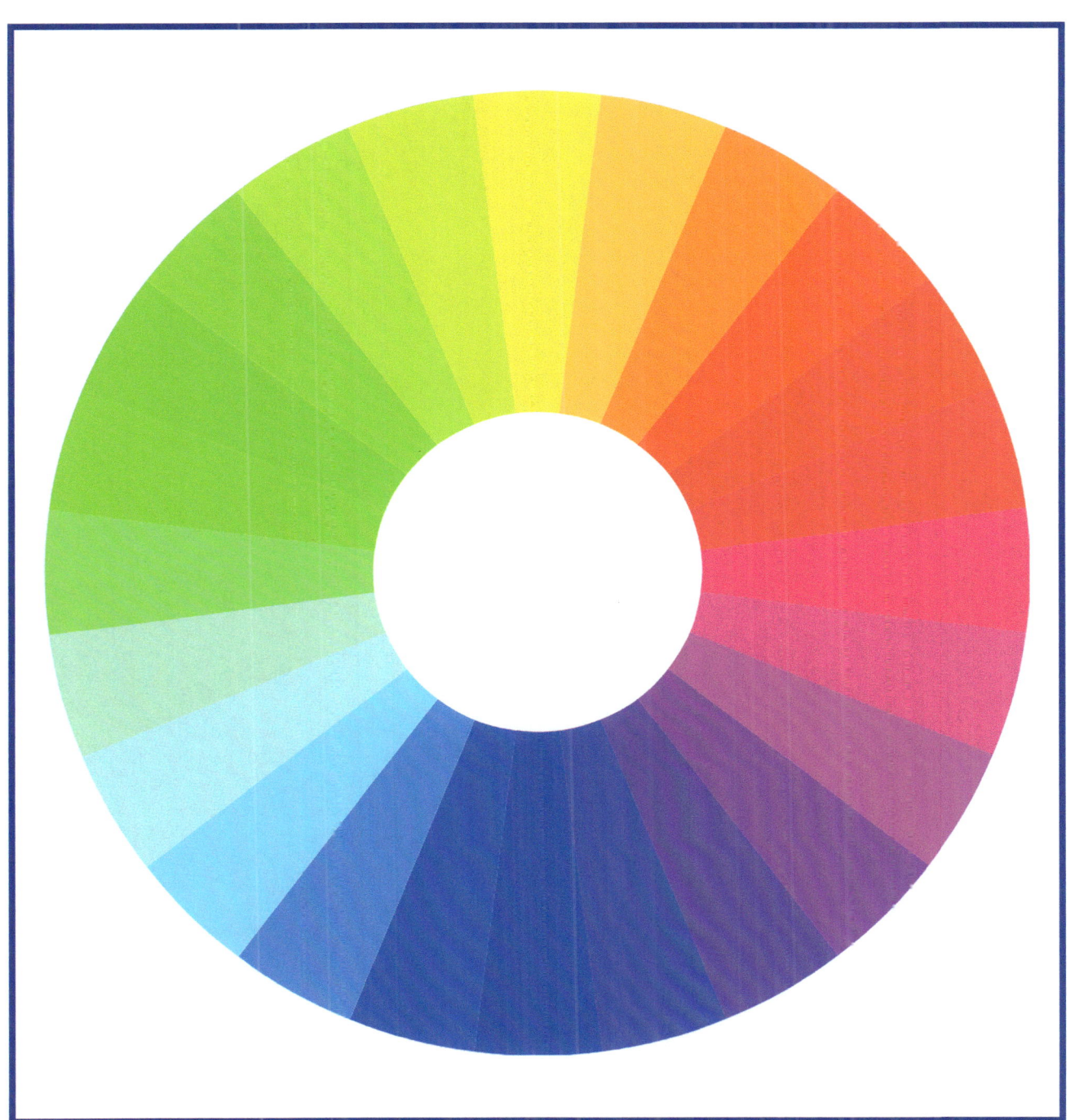

Cheat Sheet

Scan the headings and sub-headings in a text.

Ask yourself the questions **before reading**:

- **What do I want to learn?**
- **What do I think the topic is about?**

- **In which book can I find information?**
- **What page in this book?**
- **What are the pages in the book about?**

Write down the **difficult words** from the text in your note book, and find the meaning for them.

Then ask yourself the questions **during reading** the text:

- **What is the writer trying to tell me?**
- **What is important?**
- **What happens next?**

Ask yourself these questions **after reading** the text:

- **Did I understand what I read?**

Now, when we are reading a scientific text this way, we need to **check in with ourselves** now and then.

You do this by asking the following questions:

- **Am I rereading a part when I do not understand it?**
- **Am I finding difficult words?**

Once you have read the text, you should **form your opinion** on the text:

- **Do I like what the author said? Why/Why not?**
- **Are the examples clear? Why/Why not?**

AWESOME!

YOU DID IT!

YOU FINISHED
BOOK 1: ANCIENTS

Your feedback matters to us!

Tell us how you REALLY feel about our program